Pipe Lids
and
Hedgehogs

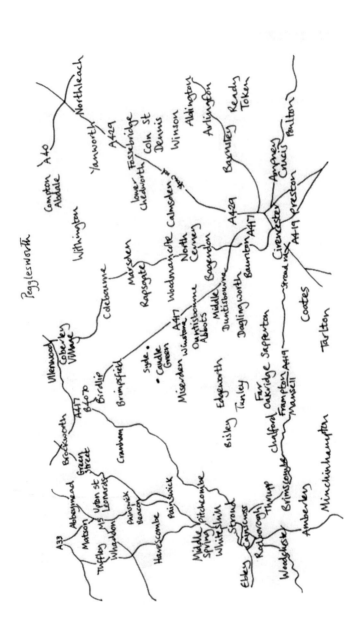

Local sketch map (*Kitty Lawson-Thomas*)

Pipe Lids
and
Hedgehogs

A Life in the Cotswolds and
a War Abroad

G Stewart.

Gerald Stewart

First published in the United Kingdom in 2009
by Frederica Freer Publishing

ISBN 978-0-9563798-0-1

Produced by
The Choir Press, Gloucester
www.thechoirpress.co.uk

Contents

List of Illustrations and Photographs

For my grandchildren
Stephen and Emily Stewart

Acknowledgements

I should like to thank the following for their help in many ways:

The Dowager Duchess of Devonshire for kindly writing the Foreword; her daughter, Lady Emma Tennant for generously funding this publication; Frederica Freer for suggesting that I write the book and subsequently editing it; Stephen Freer, Dr. Sebastian Halliday and Dr Joan Sadler for reading it over and making suggestions; Richard Beal for providing the front cover photograph, as well as other photographs, and for his financial acumen; Kitty Lawson-Thomas for the sketch map; Miles Bailey, publisher, for helpful advice; and, lastly, my wife Gladys who has patiently encouraged me over the past three years whilst I was writing this book.

Gerald Stewart
Caudle Green
August 2009

Foreword

I am delighted to write a foreword to this book for several reasons, having known Gerald and Gladys Stewart since my sister Pam Jackson bought Woodfield House in Caudle Green in 1959 and became their nearest neighbour. No one could have appreciated Gerald's knowledge of plants, gardening and the land more than she did.

Now we have the account of his long life, all lived within a few miles of where he was born, written with his razor-sharp memory. We have all seen books describing country childhoods, but usually they are by observers. This one is the real thing. Gerald's own experiences are so well written with little touches that strike the reader as coming from a son of the soil who understands all things natural. He was brought up with them and has the ability to explain them to the uninitiated.

It is our luck that he decided to write this book for his grandchildren, as the changes in the world of agriculture have been so immense during his lifetime that children of today will be able to learn from his accounts of how things were.

For those interested in the local history of this part of the

Cotswolds, they have a guide to the trades carried out in the small hamlets, starting with the Duntisbournes. His description of going to Cirencester with the carrier is vivid; being put by her to sit in a corner of the pub with a glass of lemonade while she and her cronies drank stout and swopped gossip at the bar. You feel you have been sitting there with them.

In 1943 he was called up and joined the Gloucester Regiment. His account of the landings in France in June 1944 is as chilling to the reader as it must have been for him – all told in a matter of fact way and in the spirit of his duty to King and country.

After the end of the war he joined the renowned building firm of MJ Partridge in Birdlip and became a roofing tiler working with the small Cotswold stone tiles. He was a skilled craftsman whose services were keenly in demand.

The author retired in 2000, but still finds time to look after the Woodfield House garden and its flowers and vegetables. My sister Pam would be so delighted to know that they are as well tended as ever. And so Gerald's story continues. His happy marriage to Gladys and his contented outlook are wonderful antidotes to the trials and tribulations of the world today.

Deborah Devonshire
2 September 2009.

Chapter 1

My Family

It was at Bookers, formerly known as the Poorhouse, in the parish of Coberley, that I was born on Wednesday, 29th April, 1925. I was the fourth child and third son of my father, James Birnie Stewart, and of my mother, Ada Stewart, née Coles. My brother, Philip had also been born there in 1923.

At this time, my father was employed by Major Winterbottom as a carter at Dolman's Farm, Coberley, where they also had a pedigree herd of Hereford cattle. Later that year, I was christened at St Michael's Church, Brimpsfield, by the then Reverend Wyndham Earee, my godmother being my grandmother, Clara Coles, née Preston. My godfathers were my father, and my mother's eldest brother, Frederick Coles. I never knew my uncle Frederick as he died not long after my christening and was buried between the first two yew arches on the right in Brimpsfield churchyard.

How did I come to get the name Gerald? Some years before I was born, my grandfather had been gamekeeper on the Cowley Manor estate for Sir James Horlick, who was one of the brothers who were the founders of the beverage of that name. During my grandfather's time as keeper on the

Christmas Greetings from
Gerald, 1929

estate, my grandmother worked as a daily help in the
manor. Sir James and Lady Horlick's youngest son was
named Gerald. During the time that my grandmother
worked at the manor, she grew very fond of Gerald, who
was to die quite young while serving with the army in
Egypt. My grandmother took a long time to get over his
death so, when my mother gave my grandmother the choice
to choose a name for me, without any hesitation it was
Gerald that she chose. I only hope that I have grown up to
be the person she hoped that I would be.

In 1926, we moved to a cottage at Pegglesworth where
my sister, Monica, was born, the district nurse riding her
bicycle from her home in Andoversford to attend to mother
on the birth of my second sister. My eldest brother Derrick,
having started school at Coberley, now had to walk to
school at Dowdeswell, which was quite a walk for a seven-
year old boy.

Derrick grew up to be quite a good scholar, and also a
very good cricketer. Joining the Royal Navy at the age of

thirteen, he spent the whole of his working life in, and for, the Navy, being discharged on reaching the age limit for Navy personnel. He died at the age of eighty-three at Gosport, Hampshire, his ashes being placed in the family plot at St Peter's Church, Duntisbourne Abbots, where my grandparents, and also my father and mother, are buried.

Chapter 2
Childhood

1927-1928. We are now living at Watercombes, where my father works on the Combend Estate, and it is here that my earliest memories begin. My father, having been born in the year 1881 at Forfar, County Angus, was the son of Alexander Birnie Stewart and Helen Stewart, née Drydon.

The family, 1931

My father smoked a pipe with a lid on it. This pipe lid was of great sentimental value to him! I remember it well. It was very bright, probably made of nickel plate, and had three holes in it. Engraved on it was the most perfect Scotch thistle head. One evening, he came home from work quite upset as he had lost this pipe lid on the way back from the farm. He said to Philip and myself, "When I have finished my meal, I want you two boys to come with me to see if we can find my pipe lid". So we set off across the fields, retracing his footsteps. I remember being well out in front and just before I got to the first stile, there was this little object shining in the grass. I ran forward and picked it up. It was the pipe lid! As my father jumped down off the stile, the jolt must have sent the pipe lid flying off the pipe. I ran back to give it to my father, who in return picked me up and

Gerald, 1931

Gerald and Philip catching
minnows, *c.* 1936

smothered my face with kisses, he was that pleased. I have
never forgotten that moment and, even today, I can lie back
in my chair, shut my eyes, and think of that moment and
believe it or not, I can feel my father's unshavened face
against my face.

In the valley below our cottage were the ruins of an old
bone mill. My father came home one day and said that there
were a lot of young hedgehogs down by the mill. Philip, for
whatever reason, said to me, "Let's go and get some of
them". Mother gave us a carrier bag each. I remember them
well; they were made of thick shiny brown paper, with
white sugar string handles. Where the string passed through
the bag, there was a strip of thin cardboard to reinforce the
bag. Picking up a few little hedgehogs, we then made for
home. Me, being very small, I was half-carrying and half-
dragging my bag. It was not long before the bottom of my

bag got wet, as the grass was damp, and fell to pieces, the hedgehogs falling on the ground. I just stood there, crying. Philip, who by this time was way out in front, came back to see what all the fuss was about. Seeing the bottom had fallen out of my bag, and the hedgehogs in a heap on the grass, he said, "Don't cry, Ginger. Put your hedgehogs in my bag. I will carry them home for you". Why did he call me Ginger? Because that was my family's pet name for me. In those days I had a head of auburn hair and my father's mother, although I never knew her, had a lovely head of auburn hair too, they told me, so I must have inherited it from her. This was my second early memory.

We are now living at The Pound, Winstone. The year is 1928 and my sister, Margaret, has not been long born. For a small boy who was not yet four and had lived up until now in very remote places, Winstone was a whole new world; a place full of activity. There were working farms, a blacksmith, a shop, a public house, a school, a church, and a chapel. A place that was to give me excitement and dreams.

The farm nearest our cottage was Townsend Farm, a mixed farm farmed by Mrs Cove and her son, Reg, and daughter, Molly. It was a farm full of activity the whole year round. Inside the rick yard gate was a little wooden hut in which they kept guinea-fowl as watch dogs. To anyone entering the yard, the guinea-fowl would shout, "Go back! Go back!" I remember Philip and me standing in the road, shouting, "Go back! Go back!" and, to our amusement, the guinea-fowl would answer back!

In the autumn, the rick yard would be filled with corn ricks, all built on staddle stones to raise them up out of the way of the rats. During the winter months, the threshing drum would arrive to thresh the corn. It would be driven by a portable steam engine. It seemed to me to be all belts and pulley wheels when it was working, and also labour intensive. The noise and the dust is something never to be forgotten.

Next door, was Gaskill's Farm. It was farmed by Frank Cove, Mrs Cove's son, but it was farmed as a separate unit, much of the farm income coming from Frank's job as a horse dealer. In the early 1960's, I did odd jobs for Frank; in the summer evenings, over a glass of beer, he would tell me tales of his dealing days. In the early days, his parents were farming Giboa Farm on the Earl of Suffolk's Charlton estate, near Malmesbury. Being discharged from the army in 1919, he decided to go into horse dealing, buying his first working horse soon after, and paying for it with gold sovereigns which he carried in a chamois leather bag. Horse dealers in the 1920's and 1930's were the equivalent to the car salesmen of today and he said that, the same as today, you had to beware of some of the dealers. To stand in the doorway of the blacksmith's shop and watch Ray Barrett making horseshoes, or repairing broken farm implements, the heat from the red hot metal and the sparks flying off it, was thrilling to watch; the ringing sound of metal against metal: a scene and sound like this you never forget.

Sitting on the wall at the top of our garden in the sunshine, watching a man with a Cambridge roller pulled by a heavy horse taking great strides to keep up with it, and rolling the newly-planted corn, was a sound that was music to my ears, with the skylarks rising up into the clear blue sky, singing as they ascended until almost out of sight.

Chapter 3

Schooldays

But all these pleasures were to end when, at the age of four and a half, mother said that it was time for me to start school. How well I remember my first day at Winstone C of E school! My eldest sister, Evelyn, took me down.

At four and a half, a child is normally small, but I was very small. As I walked down the classroom, the other children were sat at their desks. I heard one say, "Here comes the mighty atom." I have always believed that it was Rupert Cove that made this remark. I have no other memory of my time at Winstone school. I also went to Sunday school. The only memory I have of this is at the start of each year we were all given a stamp album, and each Sunday we were given a stamp which was a picture of a scene and contained a text from the Bible. I still have my albums.

In 1930, we moved to Box Cottage, Duntisbourne Abbots, which was to be our family home for over sixty years.

It was after we moved to Duntisbourne Abbots that I remember seeing my first steam-roller. The country roads that were made of rolled broken limestone were now being resurfaced with tar and chippings, the granite chippings coming from the quarries at Wickwar and Chipping Sodbury.

The chippings would be brought some time before and placed in heaps at intervals along the road that was to be resurfaced. By each heap was placed a 40 gallon barrel of tar. Resurfacing these roads was very labour-intensive. There would be men trimming the sides of the road, sweeping with what were to me very large stiff brushes, making sure there were no loose stones or dust before applying the hot tar. The tar was heated in what was known as a tar barrow. This was a large round metal barrow on four cast-iron wheels with a fire box underneath, a chimney stuck up front, with a man-operator hoist on top for lifting the full barrel of tar to be poured into the barrow, the whole lot being pulled by a horse.

When the tar reached the required temperature, men would draw the tar off in special containers from a tap at the rear, the containers being like large spouted watering-cans. They would then pour it onto the newly-prepared road surface where men would spread, very evenly, the granite chippings. Then would come the time that gave me such a thrill: the roller-driver would open the throttle and move the roller forward – all 8 tons of it! The smell and noise and the power, – yet it moved forward and back at less than a man's walking pace. How well I remember that roller! The motif on the front was a prancing horse and beneath it was a scroll with the word INVICTA, all in brass and highly-polished, as were the copper and brass pipes. The whole roller was cleaned down with oiled cotton waste, the roller-driver taking great pride in the condition of his roller.

It was in August of this year that my youngest brother, David, was born in Gloucester Royal Infirmary, making our

family complete. I carried on with my schooling at Duntisbourne C of E school. The school had two classrooms: one
for the infants, the other for the seniors. I started in the
infants class at the age of five. Our teacher was a Miss
Gardener who came every day from Stratton. I was born
left-handed, the only one in our family history, and it was
Miss Gardener who forced me to write with my right hand
as she said it was not correct to write with the left hand.
This gave me all sorts of problems, the worst being that I
developed a stammer which took many years to rid myself
of and, though I now do everything left-handed, I find it
impossible to write with my left hand. One point of interest: in a later school year I got to the area finals of the
national school handwriting competition. The seniors were
taught by the head teacher, Miss Pollard. I remember her as
being a big person with her long hair done up in a bun at
the back, Queen Victoria style, in a dark brown cardigan,
which she always wore open and seemed to wear throughout the year, whatever the weather. She always used pure
white paper handkerchiefs, which she would keep in the
pocket of her ill-fitting cardigan. When she stood up, the
pocket seemed to be somewhere down by her knees but, for
all this, it was not until years later that I realised and appreciated what a very good teacher she was. Drama was one of
her favourite subjects, and acting the plays by William
Shakespeare was always a must; poetry was also a favourite
of hers, especially the poems by John Masefield, who
became poet laureate in 1930 and for a while lived at
Pinbury Park. I had often seen him walking along the road
between Park Corner and Jack Barrow, wearing a hat with
a wide brim and a notebook and pencil in his hand.

Miss Pollard also took Sunday school; each Sunday, the
older ones would have to learn and recite to her the Collect

for that Sunday. On the third Sunday of each month, there was what was called the Children's Service in place of Sunday school; it was a service taken in church by the Rector, which I rather liked because we didn't have to learn the Collect. All parents were invited to this service and it was at this service that many of the mothers had their newborn babies christened. During the actual christening, the Rector would have all the children up by the font, and around the font, so that we would all get a good view of the christening.

On Wednesday, 6th April, 1938, I was confirmed by the Bishop of Gloucester, Arthur Cayley Headlam, in Cirencester parish church. After the service, our Rector gave us a small red communion book in which he had written the date: 6th April 1938 Leviticus VI 13, which reads:

The fire shall ever be burning on the altar: it shall never go out

Gerald at the time of his
Confirmation, 1938

I still have my little red book, but the communion services of today make it obsolete.

I took my first communion on Easter Sunday, following my confirmation. The Reverend C. H. T. Wright always took his communion services early in the morning, mostly at 7 am; we were not to eat anything before taking communion. My mother was very strict on this. How the church has changed! Later on, I took on the job of organ-blower, pumping the church organ every Sunday for morning and evening service. To pump the organ, there was a large wooden handle to the left and rear of the organ. To the side of it was a lead weight on a cord. When the bellows were full of air, the weight would be right down on the bottom mark, and on the top mark, when empty. Sometimes, to amuse myself, I would stop pumping to see how far I could risk the weight moving to the top mark and starving the organ of air. Sometimes, I would overdo it, the organ making a terrible sound through not having enough air, at which point Mrs Wright, the Rector's wife and organist, would stick her head round the corner of the organ and, in a very loud whisper, would say, "Pump, pump, pump!" I continued pumping the organ until 1942, when I joined the Home Guard. As most of the training took place at the weekends, I could no longer find time to pump the organ.

My father's parents had died before I was born, so that I only ever knew one lot of grandparents, that is my mother's father and mother, who liked to be called Gran and Grampy. Grampy was a tall man, always standing and walking very upright, even up to his death. He was also very bald, not having one single hair on his head. Gran was everything that a grandmother should be, and more. She had so much love and thought for her sixteen grandchildren. I never remember her being cross with any of us.

In our summer holidays, we would often go and stay with them for a while. They were them living at The Katchbar, Birdlip. Mother would put us on the bus, which was a Bristol Blue No. 57, which ran from Gloucester to South Cerney and back several times a day. The bus stop was opposite the Five Mile House. Gran and Grampy would meet us when we arrived at Birdlip. How exciting those times were! In the mornings, we spent time playing in the fields and copse by the house. In the afternoons, Gran would take us for walks to Barrow Wake, where she would buy us an ice cream cone; or we'd go into Cranham Woods, where we would play in the drifts of dry beech leaves, calling at Birdlip Stores on the way back to buy a little treat. Sunday evenings, Gran would always take us to Brimpsfield church, walking the lane from Birdlip to Brimpsfield.

The first time that she took me, I thought we were never going to get there, yet the walk did not seem half as far on the way back. When we got to church, I was fascinated to watch the bell ringers ringing the bells. I remember one of the bell ringers in particular; he had his jacket off, shirt sleeves rolled, and was putting much effort into his bell ringing. I have always thought that this bell-ringer was Ted Partridge who, in later years, was to become my employer.

Gran's house was full of interest to me. She had many stuffed animals and birds in glass cases (taxidermy). Her glass-fronted china cabinet was a real Aladdin's cave of treasures. The one that sticks out in my mind was a porcelain cat holding a handkerchief to her eyes; on a scroll by her side were the words, "Goodbye for ever, Maud". She also had a large Aspidistra in a jardinière on a stand. There was a conservatory by the front door, in which she kept many of her house plants. There always seemed to be something in bloom throughout the year. Grampy would always have a boiled egg for his breakfast, which he would take the top off with a knife, take a spoonful of yolk out, then fill the rest of the egg up with Worcester sauce. In the evenings, he would play us tunes on his melodeon or would sit and make rabbit nets. He taught David how to make rabbit nets and he became quite an expert at making any kind of net. When Grampy died, David was given all Grampy's net-making tools.

In the 1940's, my spinster Aunt Bertha bought a cottage in Duntisbourne Abbots for my grandparents. Here they lived happily until they died, Grampy in 1948, aged 79, and Gran in 1951, aged 83 years. Both were buried in St Peter's churchyard.

Growing up in Duntisbourne were very happy days for me. We each had a job to do before we could go out to play; mine was to fetch the water from the spring, as there was no mains water in those days. At times, there would be no rain water in the butts, so that would mean I would be very busy at the water cart with two buckets and a pair of oversized yokes.

In winter, we would slide on the frozen flood waters in the Groves, and sledge on the steep banks, if there was snow. Springtime, we would spend time in what we called 'birds nesting', that is, finding nests and seeing what birds had made them, and looking for the first primrose and violet. Summertime was spent tickling trout in the deep pools in the river Frome at Bull Banks, and tree climbing. Autumn was harvest time, a time when we would walk behind the binder ready to chase any rabbit that would make a run for it, confused by the noise of the binder. We would also collect hazelnuts and conkers. On wet days, we would play in what we called The Bottom Shed, because there was a shed on top of it, which you entered from the garden above.

Philip's favourite game: he was always saying, "One day, I will become famous and the King will make me a Knight, so we must be ready for that day when it comes!" So, he would make a wooden sword, put a sack on a box for a kneeler, give the sword to me and say, "You are KING GEORGE THE FIFTH! When I kneel down in front of you, I want you to dub me as a Knight. I want you to tap me on the shoulders and, as you do so, I want you to say, 'Rise, Sir Philip!' " I often wonder if anyone ever saw us doing this? Philip turned out to be a first-class Cotswold dry stone-waller but, alas, they do not give out knighthoods for Cotswold stone walling!

The fun we had with our school mates who all had nicknames! A lot of the girls did, too. We also gave nicknames to a lot of the village elderly residents, but were careful not to let them hear us calling them by it. My sister, Monica, was a real tomboy, as they would call them in those days. She was nearly always with us boys and our mates, doing whatever we were, whether it was catching minnows and sticklebacks in the brook, making a bow and arrow, or tree climbing, she could do it and was always there with us, joining in whatever we were doing.

Chapter 4

Village Life and Village Characters

Mrs Dixey was the village carrier. Every Friday, she would drive her pony and cart to Cirencester to take or bring back any parcel required by any of the villagers, sometimes making the journey twice a week. Being the generous person that she was, I often wondered how much payment or reward she received for this service. Mrs Dixey thought the world of me and I simply adored her. She was like a second grandmother to me. Sometimes, when I was on holiday, and the Friday was fine and favourable, she would take me to Cirencester, with me sitting up in the cart beside her. She always used to wear a hat with a wide brim; it was black and made of something that looked like black shiny straw, held in place by a large hat pin or, probably, two. It was to stop it blowing off as we trotted along the main road, although we never went that fast. As we went over the cross in Cirencester, I remember seeing young men standing in groups, making conversation with each other as traffic passed by, and thinking I would like to join them when I grew up. It was only years later that it came to me that they

were some of the unemployed young men of Cirencester
and it was not their choice to be in this position. We would
drive on down to a hostelry to tie the pony up. I do not
remember which one it was but I have a feeling it may have
been The Wheatsheaf.

Then, the first place of call was Selby's, the tobacconist,
where Mrs Dixey would buy her snuff. Miss Selby would
put a little brass weight on one end of the scales, take a tin
off the shelf, and tip the loose snuff into the dish on the
other end of the scales. When it was the correct weight, she
would then tip it into a paper bag. After doing more of her
business, Mrs Dixey would go into the grocer's and buy a
large lump of cheese, then go across the road to the baker's,
where she would buy a newly-baked cottage loaf. From
there, it was into the saloon bar of The Bishop Blaize, which
was very dark and dismal, the colour of the walls and
ceiling doing very little to help matters. There, she would
push me up into the darkest corner, buy me a glass of
lemonade, and tell me to be quiet. Soon, many of her friends
came into the bar: women of similar character to Mrs
Dixey, they would all sit at the long bar table, each with a
glass of stout. It was then that Mrs Dixey would take a
knife from her bag and carve the bread and cheese into large
portions, offering it to all the women. I never remember
seeing any butter. When the meal was over, each woman
would take it in turns to pass her snuff box round the table,
and what a collection of boxes they were! All different in
size and colour. This went on until 2 o'clock closing time,
when Mrs Dixey would finish the rest of her business,
collect the pony and cart, and head back for home.

Mrs Dixey's house was one of those that seemed to have
food on the table all day long. I loved being given a slice of
her fruit cake which seemed to contain more fruit than

cake, and it also had a slight taste of the smell of the Florence oil stove in which she had baked the cake; but in those days, we were young and hungry. There was always a large brown enamel teapot on the side of the kitchen range.

Mr Dixey was a small man, making his living catching and selling rabbits, selling honey from the many bees which he kept, and selling produce from the many gardens that he rented. When at home, he would sit in his high backed chair in the corner, near the kitchen range, smoking a white clay pipe. Every so often he would put the pipe down, pick up the teapot with both hands and take a swig out of the teapot spout! Though I thought it was rather disgusting, I also thought that it was very amusing. Mr Dixey always had a pet whippet; the last one he had I remember was pure black and called Spider. When Mrs Dixey died, I lost a great friend, and the village and the Cotswolds a great country character. Where are the characters of today?

The village baker was Arthur Holland, whose bakery was down by the ford at Duntisbourne Leer. He lived in the cottage opposite, with his wife, who kept the village shop. Many of the grocery products which she sold were sold loose; very few things were pre-packed in those days: tea, sugar, rice, dried fruit and biscuits were all sold loose, as well as other things. When a customer ordered any of these things, she would weigh out the right amount, tip it into a thick brown or black paper bag, fold the top over, and tie it down with thin white sugar string.

Mr Holland did all the baking himself, delivering the bread round the villages in his bread cart, often working late into the night. He got the flour for his bread-making from Healys Flour Mill at Tewkesbury and it was delivered by a steam lorry with solid tyres, the rear wheels being driven by a large chain. On top of the cab was a name-plate which read 'Hercules'.

In later years, beginning to lose his sight, and getting bad on his feet, he decided to give up baking and turned to keeping a few cattle on some small fields that he owned.

One day, I was walking past one of his fields where he was stood looking over the gate dressed in a brown smock and trilby hat, which he always wore. Seeing me, he called me over and said, "How many kine can you see, my boy?" There were seven cattle in the field so for fun I said, "Six, Mr Holland". His reply was, "You must get your eyes tested or learn to count! I can see seven". This from a man with failing eyesight. Mr Holland suffered a tragic death. His wife died before him. Living on his own, almost blind, and very bad on his feet, he fell into the fire and got burnt to death.

Miss Ingels owned and ran the Lavender Cottage Hand Laundry from a cottage in Duntisbourne Leer, employing women workers from the villages. In the garden were many clothes lines on which the washing was hung to dry. The remainder of the garden was planted with lavender bushes, which were harvested, dried, and made into small sachets. One of the sachets would be placed in the clean laundry before being returned to the customer. Miss Ingels had a Morris motor car which the gardener would drive to pick up or deliver the laundry to her customers. To celebrate the coronation of King George VI, Miss Ingels had planted four balsam poplar trees in the meadow which she owned, planting them at a small ceremony. She named the four trees King George, Queen Elizabeth, Princess Elizabeth, and Princess Margaret. Being near the stream, the trees grew very quickly and grew very large. These trees have since been felled.

Over the wall, at the top of our cottage garden, were the

village allotments. At the far end of the allotments was a high wide hedge, and one or two mature trees. Sometimes, when I did something wrong, my parents would punish me and I would walk out on them saying, "I am running away from home!" I would then go across the allotments, finding a nice seat in the hedge and making sure no one could see me, but also making sure I could see our cottage. I would sit and wait for the search party to appear. The light fading, and no search party in sight, I would creep back home, only to hear mother say, "We didn't expect to see you tonight!" I would reply, "It was too late to go anywhere".

To celebrate the Silver Jubilee of King George V, a large bonfire was built in the field known as wych hazel, which is the first large field up the Jack Barrow road on the right. When the daylight was fading, it was set alight and, to a boy of ten, that was some bonfire! Drinks and food were given out, and celebrations took place round the bonfire. Each child was given a coronation mug. We were then also given a coronation medal. The medal was given and paid for through the generosity of Bobby Perkins, who was a Conservative Member of Parliament, his parents living at Duntisbourne House. Bobby also had an aeroplane which he kept in a hanger and flew from a landing strip on his brother Russell's farm at Jack Barrow. I remember him christening a new aeroplane with champagne outside the hanger one afternoon. Then there was the time when a pigeon fancier from Stroud challenged Bobby to a race from the Houses of Parliament: pigeon against aeroplane, the pigeon to its loft in Stroud, the aeroplane to the landing strip at Jack Barrow, Bobby going by car from the Houses of Parliament to pick up his aeroplane and flying it to Jack Barrow. Bobby took up the challenge but I cannot remember the result.

After Mr Holland gave up bread-making, Mr Workman took over his customers, supplying their bread, which he baked in the old bakehouse at the Fosse, where Mrs Bliss had once baked bread. As business improved, he had a house and what was then a very modern steam bakery built, all very up-to-date. But, in later years, he could no longer compete with the national bread-making companies, so he sold the business to Days of Chedworth and the bakery became what is now the Centurion Garage.

The milk was delivered around the village by Mr W. Evans, who had a herd of milking cows at Yew Tree Farm. He would deliver to most of the cottages, carrying the milk in two large buckets hanging from a pair of yokes, carried on the shoulder. Each bucket had a lid. Inside the bucket was a pint measure and also a half-pint measure which he used to measure the milk into the customer's can or jug, having measured out the required amount. Mr Evans would always dip the measure into the milk and tip a little extra into the can or jug.

As farming began to get more modernised, Mr Evans gave up the milk round, it being taken over by T. Holder of Winstone, whose dairy was in the buildings (now in ruins) directly opposite the Duntisbourne Abbots turning off the A417. The milk that he supplied was sold in waxed cartons, pint and half-pints sealed at the top with a metal strip. It was delivered to the village by his son, Norman, using a bicycle, with a box on the side car. Everyone remarked what good firelighters the wax cartons made!

There were three butchers who delivered meat to the village: R. & R. Hitch, T. Shilham and W. Humphries, all coming from Cirencester every week, each one having their own loyal customers.

Two coalmen delivered coal: W. Jones, who had his own

business, and a much bigger firm by the name of Farrells, whose delivery man I remember was Starling Blackwell.

There were also two vans delivering hardware goods and paraffin. The vans were owned by W. Rowe and Gilmans. A Mr Cook, who lived in Daglingworth, and who worked for the GCC, was the local chimney-sweep, sweeping chimneys in his spare time.

W. Partridge, who lived in the village and who also worked for the GCC, was the local grave-digger. Mr Judas Partridge was the local wheelwright and coffin-maker. In the yard opposite his workshop was a barn-like structure with a corrugated iron roof. The sides were clad with Yorkshire boarding which finished a few feet from the ground. In this building, he stored all the timber for his work: elm boards for coffin-making, other timber for making wheels. Each piece of timber was stacked with a space between it and the next, which allowed the air to pass and which helped to season it. Mr. Partridge's cottage was quite a way from his yard and workshop. In the dark late afternoons, when he had turned in for the evening, we found the barn was the most wonderful place to play but, also, a dangerous place, as it was quite easy to get a foot or finger trapped.

How well I remember the wheelwright's workshop! It was a moderate-sized building, having double doors at the one end and a large window to the right which was against the roadside. On our way to school, we would sneak up and take a peep at what Mr Partridge was making, trying all the time not to draw his attention, though he must at times have seen us. I seem to remember that when he was making a coffin he had a shutter which he would put up against the window, working in the shop with the double doors half-open, as death and anything to do with death was not shown or spoken about so openly as it is today. How well I remember when Judas Partridge, the wheelwright and coffin-maker, died, but not the date. On our way to and from school, we would have to walk past his cottage where the curtains at the roadside were drawn across and remained so until after his funeral. We children would tiptoe past his cottage in silence, having been taught to have respect for the dead, as well as for the living.

A big occasion for us was when the Cotswold Hunt Foxhounds would meet at the Five Mile House. A lot of us would walk up from the village to see this spectacle: grooms arriving with hunters, their masters arriving in chauffeur-driven cars, a few dressed in red [pink]coats, the women always dressed in habit and riding side-saddle, with veils over their faces. The stirrup cup finished, there would be a few words by the huntsmen with any of the landowners present and the hunt would then move off to the first draw of the huntsman, leading the hounds with the followers close behind. One or two of us lads would spend most of the day following the hunt. The general idea was to work out where the hounds would run and get in front of the follow-ers, ready to open and shut the gates, which they needed to get through. Seeing a young lad holding the gate open for them, one or two of the riders would throw a penny (some-times, two) at my feet. This did not happen every time. Sometimes, I had to be satisfied with a "Thank you", some-times a grunt. Just before dark, I would arrive home very leg-weary, but with a few pence in my pocket, saying to myself, "A day well spent."

The garden at Box Cottage was on four levels: the shed and yard at road level, the cottage and garden on the second (reached by steps from off the road). Then there were gardens on the third and fourth levels. All levels were reached by a flight of stone steps. Most people would have called these gardens terraced gardens, but my father named them Bottom Deck, and Middle and Top for gardens three and four. The whole family referred to them as decks. On either side, at the top of the steps leading to the middle deck, were two very old box trees from which I would imagine our cottage got its name. My father gave us the garden to the left of the steps, on the top deck, for a pets' graveyard. It was there that we always buried our pets when they died or had been put to sleep. In the graveyard were the graves of dogs, cats, rabbits, canaries, budgerigars, tortoises, and goldfish. They were all laid to rest at the family home, some of them even brought back after my brothers and sisters had got married and had left home, so much love was there for all our pets.

From the 1st of October until February each year, the woods on the Bathurst Estate were open for cottagers to collect firewood, the only restriction being you were not allowed to take any kind of cutting tool – axe, saw, billhook – into the woods. You could only take what wood was down on the ground, small and light enough to carry.

On Saturdays, if the weather was favourable, mother would pack us sandwiches, a bottle of cocoa (wrapped in newspaper to keep it warm) and send Philip, Monica and myself wooding up into Overly Wood. Our first job was always to load our truck with wood to take home with us. We would then spend the rest of the day picking up wood, stacking it on the edge of the wood beside the ride. We would spend many Saturdays during the time the woods were open, gathering wood so that, by the end of February, with father's help on some Saturday afternoons, we would have quite a large pile of fire wood. My father would then hire a lorry to fetch the firewood home. These Saturdays were always fun and never seemed much like work to us.

And to get home, on a cold frosty evening, to our warm cottage, where mother would have a plateful of fried sprats and slices of crusty bread off of a cottage loaf, was the icing on the cake. Oh, what simple, luxurious living this was! But, alas, the wood in which we spent so many happy Saturdays is now a cornfield.

During the early years of the war, they built an aerodrome on the field known as the Hundred Acres. It was not so much an aerodrome as a landing strip, and to increase the length of the runway, they cleared forty-three acres of wood to make room for it: the very first part of the wood in which we had spent so many happy Saturdays.

During the second World War, Aston Down was a 'bomber' station, the bombers flying from there to carry out bombing raids on Germany. Any of the bombers damaged during these raids would be flown into Park Corner so as not to obstruct the runways of Aston Down, making it difficult for other bombers to take off or land. Here, they would be towed by tractor into the woods and parked under camouflage nets, out of view of any German raider. Here they were repaired and serviced before being flown back to Aston Down, ready to carry out further raids over Germany.

Some days, we would go up and see the bombers flying in. At touch down there was always a military ambulance waiting. When the bomber came to a halt, the crew from the ambulance would enter the bomber, bringing out the casualties. It always seemed to be the rear gunner who was wounded.

One Saturday morning, there was great excitement in the village. Farmer Jacob Gibbins' hayrick, in a field on the Leachway, was on fire. The fire-brigade and police were called but, by the time the fire-engine arrived from

Cirencester, the rick was well and truly ablaze. The chief Fire Officer decided that it was too late to save any of the hay and, as there was no danger of it setting anything else on fire, it was decided to let it burn itself out. The police were already making enquiries into the cause of the fire. One of my playmates, who lived nearby, told the police officer that the night before he had seen a tramp with a moustache, and wearing a Trilby hat, settling down for the night under the hayrick. The officer asked the lad if he would recognise the tramp if he saw him again. The lad replied that yes, he would. The officer then asked him to get into the police car. For some time they drove round the lanes, looking in sheds and barns as they went but no sign of a tramp could they find. After quite a time, the lad could no longer hide his guilt, telling the officer that there was no tramp and that it was he who had set fire to the rick. I do not remember what punishment the lad received. (I could find out by asking, as my playmate is still alive and well at my time of writing, but it is better left as it is).

Mother was always very strict on table manners. Having six hungry children sitting round a large kitchen table, it must have been quite a task to keep an eye on all of us! To help mother in her teaching, she had a thin cane, which she called her Tickleback. This was always laid on the right-hand side of her place setting at meal times and, if mother spotted any one of us misbehaving before, during or after the meal, as well as a word of correction, we would feel the sting of the Tickleback, mostly on the knuckles.

The children in Duntisbourne were very well looked after as far as treats go. We were always taken to the seaside at least once a year, mostly to Weston-super-Mare. The Rector would always give the Sunday School children a summer tea party, which was held on the lawns at the Rectory, where we would have sack races, three-legged races, egg and spoon races, and wheelbarrow races. Also, a treasure hunt, which was always my favourite. We were joined at this party by the Edgeworth Sunday School children, the Rector being the Rector of the two parishes.

At Christmas, there was always the school party and another Sunday School party, as well as one given by Captain Dalton. All these parties were held in the school, as there was no village hall. The school parties would always end with some kind of entertainment, usually a conjuror, who would hold us spellbound as well as amazed. At the end of the party, we would all be sent home with a goodie bag, which always contained an orange. Captain and Mrs Dalton lived at the Windmill, both having a great love of children and getting pleasure out of giving us a tea party at Christmas. This party was always looked forward to as it was always followed by a silent film show.

Captain Dalton was very much a military man and always dressed as such. He had a military-style hair cut and, walking round the tables at the tea party, would make sure we all had plenty to eat and drink. He would say in a loud voice, "I must have a sticky bun! I just love sticky buns!" The tea party over, we would all walk up to his double garage at the Windmill for the film show. To get the right distance from projector to screen the seats, which were forms, were set up diagonally, corner to corner, across the garage. The films were all black and white, silent, but with a text beneath which we were encouraged to read aloud for the benefit of the younger ones. The reason that the films could not be shown in the school room was because there was no electricity at the school. They depended on oil lamps for lighting. Captain Dalton had his own electric light plant. Sometimes, during the film show, the engine generating the

electricity would stop, putting the garage into total darkness. But the gardener was always on standby for any
emergency, always getting the engine going again quite
quickly. We thought it was great fun to be left in the dark,
the younger ones being frightened.

At the age of thirteen, I got a job nights after school,
working in the gardens of the Rectory. One of the many
jobs I was given to do after school on a Friday during early
Spring, was picking violets. The beds in the knot gardens at
the Rectory were planted with Devonshire violets with
beautifully scented, long-stemmed blooms. The Rector's
wife would give me a flower basket, a reel of green silk
thread, a pair of scissors, telling me how many blooms and
leaves to put in a bunch, how many bunches she needed,
and leaving me to it.

On Saturday mornings, with other garden produce, she
would take it all to the W. I. stall at Birdlip, which was held
in a purpose-made wooden building which stood in the
garden of one of the cottages in Birdlip Street, somewhere
up near the shop.

Mr Gibbs farmed New Bold Farm. It was only a small
farm, so it could not carry much stock: several dairy cows,
some young stock, pigs in the pigsty, quite a flock of laying
hens, plus a lightweight cob, which he used for work on the
farm (and also for taking Mr Gibbs on business and shop-
ping trips, pulling a very smart gig).

Every summer, having no hay-making machinery of his
own, a neighbouring farmer would cut the grass and make
the hay which Mr Gibbs would put into haycocks and cart
home to be put into the stone barn at his leisure. Having no
family, this was very laborious, taking him a long time
getting all the hay into the barn. But, on Saturday afternoons, Philip, Monica (whom Mr Gibbs always called

"Moniker") and myself would help him to get some of the hay in. Late in the afternoon, we were given a break while Mr Gibbs did the milking. During this break, Mrs Gibbs would bring out sandwiches, slices of homemade cake and glasses of cool refreshing milk. The sandwiches most always contained her homemade cheese which was very soft and white in colour. Hungry as I was, I found the cheese most revolting. There was no way that I could dispose of it as she would always stand talking to us, so I had to eat it and suffer.

Picking up the hay, Mr Gibbs would load the cart, while Philip and I pitched the hay up to him. Monica's job was with a wooden hay-rake to rake any loose hay that was left behind into a heap for us to pick up. She, being a proper chatterbox, would stand by us having her say. Mr Gibbs would then shout "Moniker! Moniker! Get behind the cart and rake up the hay!" This she would do, feeling very subdued.

One afternoon, I remember, an aeroplane came flying low over us, probably from the RAF Flying School at South Cerney. We all looked up. Mr Gibbs, looked straight into the sun, which made him sneeze. He sneezed so much that his false teeth fell out! So, there he was, looking for his false teeth in amongst the hay. We all thought that it was so funny and could do nothing but stand there and laugh.

Philip was always asking if he could ride the horse. Mr Gibbs promised that when all the hay was safely in the barn, he could then have a ride. That day came. Mr Gibbs made the halter into a bridle with reins, and with no saddle, Philip got onto the horse's back. The horse took a few paces forward, and then stopped. Philip, having read in cowboy stories how the cowboys would dig their spurs into the horse's flank to get them going, did just that with the heel of his boot. The horse was not having any of this, and reared up within seconds. Philip was sat on his backside on the yard floor.

In the farmyard, there were many clumps of Rayless Mayweed. On warm, sunny days, if walked upon, it would give off the most pungent smell, a smell that you liked or disliked but a smell that I have never forgotten.

Mr Gibbs later sold up and moved to Newent where he lived until his death. Mr Young then bought New Bold Farm. His wife, being a fully qualified nurse, gave first aid to the children in the village. Any of us who got cut or grazed while playing would make our way to Mrs Young's kitchen for treatment, where she kept a large assortment of first aid kit. All this was at her own expense and used for the benefit of the village children.

Chapter 5

My First Job

April, 1939. I am now fourteen and due to leave school at the end of the summer. Fourteen years old and still unable to ride a bicycle! This was another of my problems, and which I always believed was caused by being forced to write right-handed by my school teachers. Unable to ride a bicycle was a worry for my parents, as there was very little work within walking distance of our cottage; but all their worry was over when I came home one afternoon and told them that the Rector had given me a full-time job in the gardens of the Rectory!

My working hours were to be from 8 am–5 pm, Monday to Friday and from 8–12 noon on Saturday. For this I would be paid 10 shillings per week, which is 50p in today's money. It was quite a cut in wages from the 6 pence an hour he paid me for the hours that I worked after school. I never did really figure this out. My work at the Rectory was quite variable. One regular job was to clean the Rector's car, which was a large black Rover, and his daughter Betty's Morris Convertible.

The cellar beneath the Rectory was quite large, consisting of a series of compartments. The only access to the cellar

was by way of stone steps from the outside. In the compartment near to the entrance of the cellar were two large cast
iron Robin Hood solid fuel boilers, one for heating the
domestic hot water, the other heating the water for the
central heating. They were fired on a mixture of coke and
anthracite. Every year, the Rector would have a load of each
delivered and stored in the cellar. A load of coke would be
tipped down the chute into the cellar. My job was then, with
a wheelbarrow, to wheel the coke into one or two compartments. Having finished this, another load of anthracite
would be delivered and tipped down the chute to be
wheeled into further empty compartments. When the
boilers were in use, the fuel would be mixed fifty/fifty and a
small amount at a time would be wheeled and tipped up
into the compartment near to the boilers. What a dirty,
dusty job this was! The fuel was mostly delivered in the
summer time, when the weather was hot, making matters
worse.

The Rectory had its own acetylene gas plant which
provided the lighting in the Rectory. The plant was housed
in a purpose-built stone building near to the main building.
The plant consisted of four cylinders, coupled together, but
each one could be used separately. Inside each cylinder was
a metal basket, the same size as the inside of the cylinder.
These were perforated with many holes. It was into these
baskets that the lumps of carbide were put. The lumps of
carbide were on average the size of a small hen's egg. These
lumps varied in colour from a brown to almost a black,
depending on which company supplied it.

They came in airtight drums containing one hundred-
weight. When the gas plant was in use, two cylinders would
supply the gas needed, with the remaining two in reserve.
Should ever the gas supply run out, the Rector would bring

the two cylinders that were in reserve into use. When the carbide was fully spent, it turned into a pure white putty-like material. This was tipped into a purpose-built vault outside the gas house and the basket refilled with fresh carbide. The vault would be emptied during the winter when we would wheel the spent carbide onto some waste ground and bury it.

The Rector, with his two friends, the Reverend Mr Hughes, who was Rector of Upton St Leonards, and his brother, Dr Hughes, who had a practice in Cirencester, rented a mixed shoot over farm land at Coln Rogers. Shooting days were mostly Thursdays, between September and February. Each partner would invite a guest in turn every third week, making it four guns each week that they had a shoot. The Reverend Mr Hughes' gardener and myself were employed as beaters, plus several men from the village. Partridges were always driven, but the rest of the shoot was what is called a "walk up shoot", where guns and beaters walk forward together but at a safe distance apart, beaters having the job of carrying anything that they shot.

On shooting days, everyone would meet up at the farm buildings which stood on the Barnsley side of the Barnsley to Coln Rogers crossroads. Plans for the day's shoot would be discussed. We would then move to the part of the estate where the day's shoot would begin. Lunch times, we would all meet back at the farm buildings, from where we started for a picnic lunch. Miss Marchant, the Rector's cook, always made me a picnic in a basket, and always added a small bottle of lemonade. I remember some Thursdays, on real cold winter days, the lemonade would be as cold as ice. My teeth being very sensitive, to drink this lemonade would set off toothache which would continue for most of the afternoon.

At the end of the afternoon's shoot, everyone would meet back at the farm buildings, where the local beaters were paid off. The day's bag was laid out and counted. The guns took their requirements and what was then left was put into a hamper to be taken to the game dealer, and sold to help pay for some of the shoot's expenses.

Miss Marchant was a lovely person. In the winter time, she would say to Mr Bevan, the head gardener, "My stomach is all upset. It will snow within the next forty-eight hours", and she was rarely wrong!

In 1940, the Reverend Mr Wright gave up the living of Duntisbourne with Edgeworth, so I was given notice. As a result of this, I was offered a job at the Windmill for Captain Dalton, and also a job at Church Farm for Major and Mrs Reinhold. Mr Bevan, who had already left the Rectory and now was head at Church Farm, asked me to join him there, so that's what I did, and never once looked back.

Life at Church Farm was so much different from working at the Rectory. The central heating and domestic hot water was provided by the same system as that at the Rectory, the only difference being that everything was at ground level, so there was not any of that cruel work, working in dirty dusty cellars. The lighting was provided by a Lister Start-O-Matic generating plant, which was run on diesel housed in a purpose-built engine house. There was a battery room on the side containing fifty-four accumulators which had to be checked frequently, and topped up with distilled water when necessary. The engine fuel tank also had to be kept topped up with diesel. The whole lot was new, very efficient and looked very impressive.

Church Farm had its own water supply, there being no mains water in the village at this time. The water was supplied from a borehole, and pumped by an electric pump to a supply tank which automatically shut itself off when the tank was full.

One of the many jobs that I had was window-cleaning, which I was not very keen on, or good at for that matter, often being told by Madam that I had not made a very good job of it and that I was to go over them again!

Another of the jobs I had was during the hunting season. If Mr Bangs, the groom, needed any help in or around the stables, I was on call to give him a hand. In return for this, he was supposed to give a hand in the garden during the summer when things were busy, but things were much quieter in the stables. Mr Bangs did not think much of this set up and did very little in any way to help out in the gardens. Mr Reinhold must have noticed this, as I remember one day Mr Bangs was walking down the drive when Mrs Reinhold shouted, "Bangs! Are you busy?" Mr Bangs stopped, swinging round on one heel, and replied, "Busy, Madam? I am always busy," and carried on walking down to the stables.

Every weekday morning, at 10 o'clock, I would walk down to the kitchen and pick up the list containing the fruit and vegetables required for that day. The vegetables were then placed in trugs and taken, as soon as possible, to the kitchen. They always used a large amount of spinach, as the two young daughters were brought up on spinach purée: a very healthy diet.

Chapter 6

The War Years

Normandy, Arras, Bayeux

Things went very well at Church Farm. It really was a job
to tell that there was a war on as there were still plenty of
parties in the big house and there seemed to be no shortage
of drink or any other commodities.

But, alas, 1941 ended in great sadness when the War
Office informed Mrs Reinhold that her husband, Major
Reinhold, had been killed in action on the 23rd December
during a tank battle in Libya, while serving with the 2nd
battalion of the Royal Gloucester Hussars. His parents
installed the lighting in St Peter's Church, Duntisbourne in
his memory, and also donated a bed in Cirencester Memo-
rial Hospital. The hospital is now the Registry Office.

As the years passed, everyone was getting more involved
in the war. German bombers flying over meant nights with
searchlights lighting up the night-time sky. The nearest
searchlight battery was between Winstone and the Knotch,
in the fields on the right. The night that the Germans
bombed Coventry, and destroyed the Cathedral, will never
be forgotten by anyone who saw it. No one in our family
slept that night, as wave after wave of German bombers

Home Guard, 1943. (Philip in the middle of the back row; Gerald at the end of the back row)

passed overhead, making that unforgettable droning sound. The sky was glowing red and orange, and did so until daylight dawned. (In later years, my wife and I took our two boys to see the ruins of the old Cathedral and to walk round the new one).

For me, besides my day time job, there were duties to be done in the Home Guard: training and, on one night a week, guard duty. The guard-room was in the bothy at the stables at Church Farm.

Then, in 1943, I had a letter from the War Office telling me to report to Bradbury Lines, Hereford on the 14th July. In other words, I was called up to serve both King and country. This was going to change my life forever, but a change that I can look back on with no regrets whatsoever.

Bradbury Lines was later to become Stirling Lines, the home of the SAS. Hereford, in those days, seemed to be a long way off. Transport was very restricted and what there was, was always overcrowded. Having been sent a free rail

Gerald. First day in the Army,
July 14th 1943

warrant with my calling up papers, on the 14th July I took an early bus to Gloucester, and caught a train to Hereford. On board the train were many young lads all making for Bradbury Lines. As we pulled into the station, I could see military personnel waiting on the platform. As we disembarked from the train, a sergeant with a clipboard, was calling out names of the new recruits he was expecting. We were then grouped together and taken to a waiting army truck which was to take us to Bradbury Lines. The camp was a Physical Training Unit, known in the army as a PTU. It was where we were to spend ten weeks building us up and knocking us into shape for army service.

Arriving at the camp, there were several NCO's who took us to our barrack room which was a wooden building holding thirty recruits. This was to be our home for the next ten weeks. We were each allocated a bed and locker. The Corporal, who was in charge of us, then introduced himself, telling us what to expect over the next ten weeks and, also, what was expected of us. He ended up saying,

> There is no need for me to tell you that there is a war on. None of us wanted to be here but we are, and we must make the best of it. In the months and, possibly, years to come, there will be many hard times. Also some good times. When the war is over, those of us lucky enough to return to our families, will have forgotten the bad times and will only look back on the good ones.

I often think of think of those words spoken by that Corporal on my first day in the army and how true they have turned out to be.

Over the next few days, we were marched to various parts of the camp for various things, such as our Pay Book (Part 1 and 2), identity discs, our uniform, boots, medical checks, inoculations, vaccinations and last, but by no means least, to the camp barber for a haircut – more of a scalp, than a haircut, there being only one style of cut in the army in those days. We were also told to learn our army number which seemed difficult at the time as eight digits took a lot of remembering. But it is a number that no one who has been in the services ever forgets.

Then, the training began in earnest. Gentle at first, more energetic as the weeks passed. Each squad was given a different colour; rivalry between each squad, in training and sports, was to see who was top squad at the end of each week. After ten weeks, we were given another medical. Those passed as fit were posted to various barracks for basic army training. Being passed as A1, I was posted to Norton Barracks, Worcester for six weeks' basic training, which was more like six weeks of basic hell. Step out of line and there was a sergeant ready to jump on you like a ton of bricks. I think that a lot of the sergeants in the army, who had never known their fathers, were sent to Norton Barracks, for they were most unpleasant people. Giving new recruits extra drills after tea was their delight, giving them great pleasure in saying, "I have nothing spoiling tonight. I don't mind staying here as long as it takes. You will get it right, even if it means staying here until lights out."

Norton Barracks was the only place during the whole of my army service where I served with members of the WRAC (Women's Royal Army Corps), a more vulgar lot of females I have never met. They were responsible for all the catering at the barracks. Each day, so many of us were detailed to report to the cook house that evening, to peel the potatoes for the next day. This in army slang was known as Spud Bashing. The duty cooks would be there and would always try to embarrass us with their language. If any of us showed any sign of embarrassment, it was just up their street. We soon learned to give back as much as we were given.

During the sixth week of training, we went before an officer who would have our personal report in front of him. After asking a few questions, he would select the branch of the service that you were most suited to. When I went up before him, he asked if my father had been in the army. When I told him that he had served throughout the first world war in the Royal Artillery, he then offered me a chance to do my time in the Royal Artillery.

Looking back, it was at this moment of time that I became the author of my own destiny in the army: the moment when I told the officer that my heart was set on serving in an infantry regiment. The officer looked bewildered at having such a straightforward request. I was then dismissed and the next recruit sent for.

Next day, all the postings were put up on the notice board. I was posted to an infantry training unit at Hyderabad Barracks, Colchester, and what a grim lot of buildings they were. They were built of red brick and looked very Victorian. Grim was hardly the word. Ten weeks in this place! What a future to look forward to! But, thankfully, after a few days, we were reselected and a platoon of us were sent to Kirkee Barracks, a very modern lot of buildings, but also a long way out from the main garrison. Here, the training was very hard, plus some nights when we got very little sleep as there was so much air activity with German bombers flying over, and the Ack Ack guns firing salvos at them.

Having completed our training, we were then posted to various infantry battalions. My posting was to the 2nd Battalion, Gloucester Regiment, which was, at that time, stationed at Blackgang, Isle of Wight. A few weeks later, the whole battalion moved to Middlesbrough, where we were to take part in the final manoeuvres, ready for the invasion of France. These were carried out in the most appalling conditions on the Yorkshire moors: rain, hail, snow, every possible sort of weather that Mother Nature could throw at us. It was so bad that the army did a rare and unusual thing: it gave orders that a rum ration should be given to all troops taking part and, to help lift our morale, Princess Alice paid us a visit. After a few more weeks' training in Scotland, the whole battalion moved to New Milton, Hampshire, where we carried out landing craft drill.

As D-Day approached, I was one of the soldiers that was selected as a reserve. We were all taken to a tented camp which was on a bombed-out site in the East End of London. It was just like a prisoner of war camp, surrounded by much barbed wire, with only one way in and one way out, and that was a heavily guarded entrance. Here, we were kept without any contact whatsoever with the outside world. We all knew what was going to happen; the only question was when?

Then, one night in June, we were marched down to the docks and loaded onto a troop ship. For some time, we were anchored just off Gravesend. By this time, I had lost all sense of time, not knowing the day of the week or even the date. Once on board, everyone was given what the army called 'bags vomiting'. They were made of strong black paper, several small ones and one large one, in which to place the small used ones. At a given time under cover of darkness, our troop ship sailed down the Thames estuary, out into the North Sea, and down the English Channel to its rendezvous position, and dropped anchor.

Once the invasion got into full swing, our ship weighed

anchor and sailed nearer the French coast and dropped
anchor at its rendezvous point. Here we waited for the
landing craft (flat-bottomed boats) that were to take us
onto the beach. The landing craft arrived at the given time
and pulled alongside the troopship. Scramble nets were
lowered into them and we were given orders to disembark
into the landing craft. In all the weeks of training we had
been given, this was one thing we had not been taught: how
to scramble down a scramble net with a full set of kit. With
the turbulent waters of the sea, it made climbing down
scramble nets very difficult; one moment, the net was verti-
cal, then it was almost horizontal, making things very
awkward. I never lost any of my equipment, but I am sure
there must have been a few who did.

The landing craft full, the scramble nets raised, we cast
off and headed for the beach, not knowing what to expect.
Would we be dropped off in deep water or, hopefully, in
shallow water? Our craft was one of the lucky ones, as it
took us right onto the beach. The ramp was lowered and we
all ran forward. The sappers had already cleared paths
through the minefields, which were clearly marked by white
tapes on either side of the path. Our orders were to keep
within the white tapes and to get clear of the beach as
quickly as possible. This we did. On reaching the assembly
point, we were loaded into trucks and driven to within a
safe distance of the place where our unit was dug in. We
then dismounted and walked forward in aircraft formation
till we reached our unit. Aircraft formation is when you
walk on the side of the road in alternate sections. Number
1 would be on the left, Number 2 on the right, 3 on the left,
and so on. The idea of this formation is to make it a more
difficult target for enemy aircraft. Thankfully, by this time
of the invasion, the German Air Force seemed to be almost

non-existent. When I reached my unit 'A' Company, 2nd Gloucester Regiment, they were dug in in an orchard just outside Tilly-sur-Seulles, a place that had seen some of the most bitter fighting. So far 'A' Company had been withdrawn from the front, and were taking a well-earned rest for a few days.

Looking around the members of 'A' Company, which I had last seen a few weeks previously in camp at New Milton, there were a few familiar faces missing but, then, this was war. It was these missing personnel that we had come to replace. It was here that our company commander, Major J. K. Lance, was decorated in the field with the Military Cross. To me, he was the finest officer in the British army; a man of great character, he had no equal. I shall never, ever forget him. On receiving his medal, he called all the soldiers of 'A' Company around him telling us that, although the medal was given to him, it really belonged to all the men of 'A' Company because it was they who had won it, and that we were to look at it as being *our* medal. He was an officer who always had the welfare of the soldiers under his command at heart, and looked on us as a big happy family, always willing and ready to sort out any soldier's problems. I did not know that day, when I rejoined 'A' Company, that later I would be stood beside the Major when he was killed. I do not wish to dwell on it too much, but I feel I must tell readers how I found the situation, there, in the battlefields of Normandy. The roads were strewn with damaged, burnt-out and abandoned military vehicles; there were many dead horses that had been used by the German military, lying on their backs, blown up like a balloon, their feet reaching skywards; there was much noise and the whine of the odd shell as it passed overhead, fired, I would imagine, at random by the German artillery, well

off target and landing well behind our lines, where it, hopefully, did no damage. In the distance, there was the
unmistakeable chatter of the Germans' best weapon, the
Spando machine gun – once heard, never forgotten. The
whole scene was one of devastation. Under the hedge, at the
bottom of the orchard, a German soldier was lying in a
shallow grave, buried, I would imagine, in haste by his
retreating comrades, the soil only just covering him, his one
hand reaching out above the soil, like a cry for help, the
blow-flies coming and going like bees round a hive in an
English country garden. In mid-summer, the sweet sickly
smell of death hung over the place. It was not a place for the
faint-hearted or those with a weak stomach.

It was here that Major Lance, our Company Commander,
promoted me to company runner, a posh name for an
errand boy. Every company had its own company runner.
The job of the company runner was to take or fetch any
written messages from Company HQ to battalion headquarters. We were given a book in which the date and time
of delivery of each item was recorded; the recipient, on
receiving the item, would sign for it. I remember taking
messages to a Captain Graham-Smith, whose initials were
R. A. On receiving the message, he would scrawl across my
little book 'Rags', thus becoming Rags by all who knew
him, a nickname which must have stuck to him for life.

Most of the time, a company runner was working on his
own and, at times, it would be very nerve-wracking. It was
at such times that I was thankful that I had been taught field
craft during my days of infantry training, as one of the foot
soldier's biggest enemy was the German 'S' mine which was
a personnel mine planted just under the surface. When
stepped on, it would spring up to about chest high, before
exploding, killing or maiming whoever stood on it.

The 2nd Gloucestershire Regiment, 2nd Essex Regiment, and the 2nd South Wales Borders made up the 56th Independent Infantry Brigade. The Brigade landed on Gold Beach on the 6th of June, with the 2nd British Army.

As the allies were advancing through France, at times at a great pace, we were taken into battle on board tanks, though not that often, thank goodness, as this did put the fear in me. The tanks that I rode on were mostly Shermans, which were not designed for this purpose. The Sherman was a battle-tank, unlike the Churchill, which was designed to carry infantry. The Sherman, being a battle-tank, had not got much that you could hang on to. Sometimes, you could be lucky as some of the tanks had extra armour welded on the outside (worn-out track). This often gave you a place to put your feet and hang on to. What a relief when the tanks stopped and we could bale out, as they say. When riding on tanks, you are left to the mercy of the gods, whereas walking into battle, you could hear the mortar, field guns, or machine guns being fired. Appropriate action could then be taken, lying flat on the ground or taking shelter in a shell-hole, which was not always handy.

When the Liberation Army broke out from the bridge-head, and was quickly advancing up through France, the 56th Independent Brigade was transferred to the 1st Canadian Army. One of its first tasks on joining the Canadians was the task of liberating the port of Le Havre, which had been by-passed by the rest of the allied forces.

Chapter 7

Le Havre

A Sunday Remembered

It was on the eve of 10th September, which was my grand-father's birthday. In perfect weather, the assault to take Le Havre began moving across the open countryside under a creeping barrage laid down by the big guns of two Royal Naval ships, which I believe were HMS Ajax and HMS Achilles, and which were anchored in the English Channel, just off Le Havre, and supported by heavy armour. We had not made much ground when our headquarters came under heavy mortar fire. The Germans, though completely surrounded on all sides, and with no means of escape what-soever, were determined to make a fight of it, and were going to go down fighting, which was ridiculous, really. Major Lance, our company commander, quickly weighed up the situation, giving orders to make for the open ditch which lay just ahead of us. But it was too late for some of us. All I remember was a loud bang, and lying there, utterly confused, the blood soaking through my battledress trousers and a burning sensation in my right thigh. I took out my field dressing and placed it the best I could on the wound to stem the bleeding. A thousand things must have crossed my mind as I lay there, amid the noise and action, my great fear being, "Would the drivers of the tanks that were moving forward see me lying there?" as I pressed my whole body as close as I could to mother earth, to avoid being hit with more shrapnel, which was a possibility. Being me, I am sure that I offered up a prayer for all of us. Then, for a while, all seemed calm and as though my prayer was answered. Stretcher-bearers arrived, lifted me onto a stretcher, placed it onto a jeep, which was then driven some way from the battlefield to a waiting field ambulance. I was then put into the ambulance with other wounded, and driven to the 8th Canadian Field Hospital, which was somewhere near to Rouen. Here, I was operated on to remove the shrapnel and made comfortable. After a few days, I was taken with others by ambulance to the 110th British Field Hospital, which was near the town of Bayeux, where I was nursed back to health by members of Queen Alexandra's Nursing Association.

After a few weeks, and once again able to walk unaided, I was sent with others to an army convalescent unit, which I believe was near the town of Arras. Here, we did all manner of things, helping each other to full fitness. Each weekend, there was a medical check on the fitness; those who passed were discharged and returned to their units.

At this point, I must mention that on the 19th May, 2008, I had an appointment at the Radiology Department at Cheltenham Hospital, where I was to be given an MRS scan. With the appointment letter, there was a questionnaire which I was asked to fill in before attending. The last question was, "Have you ever had a bullet or shrapnel wound?" Not wanting everyone to know my history – that I had been wounded – I decided not to answer this question but, for whatever reason, at the very last moment, my better judgement told me to answer "Yes" to this question. Having sat

Army report of Gerald wounded, September 10th 1944

in the waiting-room at the Radiology Unit for some time, I was called up to go to the X-Ray Department where they were to X-ray the wound. This done, I was sent back to the waiting-room. After a while, I was called into the room where the scan should have been taken; here, they explained to me that they could not give me a scan as I still had shrapnel – two pieces – in my thigh; they then showed me the X-ray plates, clearly showing two pieces of shrapnel in my right thigh. It was then explained to me that they could not under any circumstances give me a scan and were sending me home until such time as they could find a away to do it.

On 29th July, I was called back to the Radiology Department where I was given a head scan which proved negative. Why, after 64 years, has my body not rejected this metal?).

Every week some soldiers were leaving, whilst others would be arriving. I felt like the forgotten soldier, as there was never any suggestion of my leaving to join my unit. Maybe, it was because I made myself useful in various ways — helping out with jobs on the camp — that they would have liked me to become a member of staff. But, the day came when I felt it was time that I made it back to the Glosters, though I knew well the risks I would be taking. I had an interview with the officer who was in charge of the convalescent camp, telling him how happy and well-treated I had been here. I do not remember his reply, but over the next few days, and after staying in various camps, I found myself in Holland with the 'A' Company of the Glosters.

Here, I met up with Ted Castle, one of the stretcher-bearers who had given me first aid and carried me off the battlefield that September evening. It was here that he told me some very sad news, which was that Major Lance, our company commander, had died of wounds as we lay not that far apart that September evening. 'A' Company had lost a great friend, the British Army, a great leader. We had lost a man who treated humans as humans. A real gentleman in every sense of the word. Even now, as I look back, it makes me so sad, but also thankful to have known him.

Ted and I became great friends: whenever he was on leave, he always spent part of it with my parents and family, so much so that he almost became part of the family. On leaving the army, he joined the Leicestershire police force, where he remained until he retired. For one of his hobbies, he took up painting. How thrilled I was when in 2001 he gave me a painting of the family home in Duntisbourne where he had spent a lot of his free time. It is hanging on the wall in our sitting-room. At times, I sit and look at it and memories come flooding back: as a five-year old boy, leaving for school, where I would stammer and stutter through lessons; as an eighteen-year old, leaving to become a soldier to do his duty for King and country; and that sad September evening when everyone lost a true friend, Major J. K. Lance.

Moving up through Holland, we eventually arrived in an area that was known as the Island. That is the area of land that lies between the river Waal at Nijmegen and the river Rhine at Arnhem. Here we dug in at a place called Elst, where I spent my twentieth birthday. This concludes the first quarter of my life.

Chapter 8

Towards the end of the War

Holland, Germany, Bermuda, British Honduras, Belize and Jamaica

It is early May now. The war is beginning to reach its end, with the allied forces advancing on all fronts. And it was in May, under the cover of darkness, and a gun barrage laid down by the guns of the artillery, that we crossed the river Rhine in amphibious armoured vehicles to take the town of Arnhem, the scene of all that fighting and loss of life. Things were much different this time. Most of the German soldiers seemed to have lost the will to fight. There were just the odd fanatics, who needed watching. We seemed to be overrun with prisoners, far more of them than there were of us. We had got to Amersfoort, when the surrender came, amidst much joy and celebration.

In the coming days, it was a case of organising the disarming of the German soldiers; as they had so much equipment, this was a big task. I always remembered, though, that they were a defeated army. They marched into the POW camp that had been set up to take them in a very soldier-like manner. Their senior military commanders stood at the entrance to the camp, saluting each unit as it marched past to become prisoners of war, many singing German battle songs. I remember seeing the Dutch people in the town of Utrecht rounding up the women who had been socialising with the German military, if that is the correct word, running them down the streets into the town square, where amidst much jeering and cheering, their heads were shaved until they were absolutely hairless.

From Holland we moved to Germany, to a place called Bad Sassendorf. From here, we spent our days and nights patrolling in vehicles around a large area. I remember seeing German soldiers on the road, walking home. It seemed to me that when the war ended, they were just abandoned by those in charge and told to make their own way home.

One of the places where we did an hourly patrol was the Möhne Dam (the dam of the dam-busting fame). What an engineering achievement the dam was! The sheer size of it! The whole dam was covered with steel wire netting. The netting was made up of steel wire rings, some six inches in diameter, welded together and held aloft by steel girders, which held the netting quite some distance above the dam; quite a real work of art! But they shut the stable door after the horse had gone, to give some idea of how big the stretch of water was that the dam held back. This was June 1945, and the locals were saying that it still was not up to the level it was when Guy Gibson's dam-busting squadron breached it.

After various stations, the Glosters were sent to Berlin to replace one of the guards battalions which had been sent back to England to do duties. Everyone should know that at the end of the war, Berlin was divided into sectors: British, American, French and Russian. To get to Berlin by road, rail or air, you had to use what was called 'The Corridor'. The land on either side of it was policed by the Russian army. If anyone was found outside The Corridor, it meant imprisonment.

To get to Berlin by road or rail, you had to pass through Checkpoint Charlie, as it was nicknamed. Here, every one and everything was checked out by very mean-looking Ruskies, as we called them. Some days, they would let you go straight through; some days, for no reason whatsoever, they would delay you for hours on end. They never, ever seemed to be friendly towards us.

Life in Berlin was very easy for me; it seemed that we were there for no other reason than to say that a part of Berlin was under British occupation. Days were spent training with drills and lectures and not much else. In the evenings, we would visit the local cafés or take a ride into the city to Alexander Place where there was a large NAAFI (a place where you could buy almost anything).

The Russian soldiers whom we met in Berlin were so much friendlier than those mean-looking soldiers we had had to deal with at Checkpoint Charlie. They were always wanting to make conversation, almost making us feel that we were their superiors. They all seemed to look the same to me, dressed in large, round, flat-topped hats, which looked several sizes too big, and which were covered in gold braid. Their uniforms were also covered in gold braid, with many brass motifs. We were told that they were the pick of the Russian Army, which I quite believe.

After some time in Berlin, the whole battalion was called together and told by the Adjutant that we were leaving Berlin and returning to England where we would be kitted out before being sent to the Caribbean.

Having arrived back in Reservoir Camp in Gloucester to

be kitted-out with our Tropical kit, if not on duty at the
weekend, we were given a weekend pass from Friday afternoon until 23.59 pm on Sunday. We would catch the bus,
No. 57, from the centre of Gloucester, which ran to
Cirencester and on to South Cerney. And we would catch
the same bus back late Sunday evening, leaving Cirencester
Market Place some time about 10 pm for Gloucester.

Some of the lads lived in Cirencester; others in local
villages. On the Sunday evening they would all meet up in
the public bar of The King's Head for a few beers before
catching the last bus to Gloucester. I would catch the No. 57
at the Five Mile House and join my mates who, by now,
were in a jovial mood. And, nature being what it is, by the
time we got to Birdlip, my mates were suffering some
discomfort. So, Private (Rasher) Scrivens (no one seemed to
know his Christian name), would walk up to the front of
the bus and ask the driver to stop at the first lay-by –
Barrow Wake or down Crickley Hill. The bus would stop
and all the lads would make for the door. A few minutes
later, they would all be back on board, and Rasher would
shout, "OK. Take it away, driver" and we would continue
for Gloucester. We mostly had the same driver on the
Sunday night so, in the end, he would stop, by habit, but
Rasher would still count our mates on board before shouting, "OK, driver. Take it away!"

We left Southampton on board the troopship 'Carthage'.
Many of the soldiers' families were on the quayside to cheer
and wave "Bon Voyage" as we were about to sail. We were
all crowded on the top deck, shouting and waving in reply.
It really was a sight! Then, above all the noise and celebration, a loud voice boomed out. It was the Regimental
Sergeant Major, telling us to behave like soldiers, not children! His words that day were, "Anyone would think that

this was Epsom Downs on Derby Day!" I must admit that that was what it looked and sounded like.

We had a very bad trip around the Bay of Biscay; there were times when I thought the ship was going to topple over. Rough was hardly the word to describe the raging sea but, with a prayer and words of comfort from crew members, mercifully we made it to calmer waters. I, for one, was most thankful for this.

We then sailed for Bermuda, the sea never being that angry. In fact, twice I remember it being as still as a mill pond. One of my biggest disappointments was seeing the Flying Fish. Having heard about them as a schoolboy, I did not really know what to expect but I do know that I expected them to be bigger than they were. They looked no bigger than pilchards, sparkling silver as they flew between the roll of the waves. Another of my boyhood dreams sadly exposed.

As our troopship approached Bermuda, the view that we had was really stunning. All the white villas and apartments, and the pure blue sky reflected in the blue sea. This was a real haven. We docked in the port of Hamilton, the reason being that we were to leave a detachment of soldiers to man the garrison on the island. Other than the soldiers who were to take over the garrison duties, the remainder of us were not allowed off the ship. But, they allowed fruit-sellers to come on board. I remember paying one shilling for an orange – that was 12 pennies in old money. On making enquiries about the price, the excuse was that everything had to be imported to the island, therefore making the cost of living very high. (Last February, 2008, the man in the market in Cirencester offered me 5 oranges for a pound. A bargain, he called it. It had taken 60 years for the Bermuda prices to catch up here, in the UK!)

From Bermuda, we set sail for British Honduras and the port of Belize, where we were to drop off a detachment of soldiers. Here things were different. The harbour at Belize was unable to take a ship the size of 'Carthage'. We dropped anchor some way out and smaller craft were used to transfer troops and equipment ashore. In the meantime, all we could do was to sunbathe and take in the scenery: palm trees, silver sand on the beaches, and wonderful blue skies. I remember how clear the water was and seeing the barracudas swimming round the rear end of the ship, ready to take any scraps coming from the galley. I well remember, too, one of the seamen trying to bait one with a large lump of raw meat on a length of cord. I never saw what the result was as the meal call sounded and I, for one, was not going hungry.

Weighing an anchor, we then set sail for our final destination: the port of Kingston, Jamaica. Sailing across the Caribbean Sea was quite exciting for me. The amount of flotsam and jetsam in the water was unbelievable: palm leaves, coconut shells, coconut outer cases, and no end of debris. We knew that we were in a whole new world and I found myself reciting John Masefield's poem, 'Ships'. When learning that poem as a boy, never once did I ever think that I would be sailing through the tropics!

Arriving in Kingston harbour, we were greeted by many small local boys asking for pennies. The idea was to throw the pennies into the water; they would then dive down and retrieve them, never once missing one. We disembarked from the ship which had been our home for many weeks, and were taken to Up Park Camp, which was the army barracks. The barracks was made up of rows of wooden huts, each with its own veranda between avenues of mango trees, which seemed to be prolific the year I was there. The whole camp was surrounded by a 6' metal fence on top of a 3' high stone wall. For us, there was no means of escape.

For the first few nights, we were all kept awake by the crickets out on the veranda. We found that the only way to stop them was to throw cups of water into the inside of the roof of the veranda. This task fell on the one who was most annoyed. Up Park Camp was to be my last station before leaving the army.

The army had cheated on all us National Service men, that is, those who had been called up in the early part of the war. On joining the army, you were given an army Pay Book, Part 1 and Part 2. Part 1 carried all of your personal details: date of birth, birthmark, if any, nationality, religion, weight in pounds, height in inches, medical grade (A1, B2 or C3), records of all inoculations and vaccinations, all lengths and types of leave and, most important of all, length of enlistment. This is where I think that the army cheated us National Service lads. The day that we joined the army, the length of enlistment was put down in our Pay Books as being 'Duration of War.' A few months before the invasion of France, all conscripts had to hand their Part 1 Pay Book into head office. Now, every barrack-room in the army has its own barrack-room lawyer. He is that ordinary fellow who tells those of us in the barrack-room our rights and entitlements. He is unpaid and self-appointed, a kind of shop steward. You will find these lawyers throughout the British Army. I well remember the day we were given our Pay Books back. Our barrack-room lawyer spotted that they had stamped out 'Duration of War' and, in place, had stamped in an indelible stamp the bold letters 'D of E' (Duration of *Emergency*) as being the length of enlistment. The lawyer said that someone in the War Department, or such place, had suddenly realised that the Duration of War meant that, for National Service men, the day that the armistice would be signed we all could walk out and return home. He may have been right; he could have been wrong, because I have never really been *officially* discharged.

I was discharged from the army on the 31st December, 1947, and straight away placed on Class Z Reserve from which I have never been discharged. If the army gets hard up I, with others, could be called up, as we were in 1949 for several weeks, to do what was called Z training down on Salisbury Plain at Ludgershall. Quite a waste of time, but I enjoyed meeting up with old mates and having a few too many beers.

Part 2 of the Pay Book was a record of all payments made: the amount and the date. On pay days, you would enter the office, hand your Pay Book to the clerk, who would be sat to the right of the paying officer; he would then fill in the amount payable, passing the book to the officer, who would put the amount payable on the book, pushing it to the front of the desk. You would then take two paces to the right, salute the officer, pick up the book and cash, do a smart turn to the right and march smartly out of the office. My starting pay was 3 shillings a day. The army was on a seven-day week at that time.

Chapter 9

The End of the War

Army Life in Jamaica

Now, a little about life in the army in Jamaica. Firstly, it was hot. Today was hot, yesterday was hot and you knew that tomorrow would be hot! But, it made very little difference to the army. We carried out our duties the same as we would have done in a more friendly climate. One of our duties was to guard the Governor's Palace, which was a wonderful, large white building, set in the most beautiful surroundings. Kingston Park race course ran down one side of the grounds; if you were lucky to be on duty on a day of the races, you could get a good view of horse and jockey as they went thundering by, which could be quite exciting. We often played sports against sailors whose ships had called into port for a few days. Sea-bathing was very restricted, only doing so where there were signs saying it was safe. These places were far and few between. The reasons for all this were that the waters around the island were very deep in places, and the beaches on much of the island, instead of sloping gradually to the seabed a few hundred yards from the shore, suddenly dropped into very deep water and the current could take you under the shelf. There was no escape.

Kingston town had its own various quarters: Spanish Town, etc. All military personnel were banned from Hanover Street, which was the red light district. The wild life that interested me were the chameleon lizards (how they changed colour to match their surroundings!) and the humming birds as they gathered nectar from the flowers. Then, there were scorpions. Every morning you had to make sure and tap your boots on the floor, as there was always the possibility that one may have crept into the boots overnight, and they carried the most unpleasant sting in their tail.

At night, we were made to sleep under mosquito nets, though the mosquitoes were not known to carry malaria, as mosquitoes do in the Far East.

The local daily newspaper was *The Daily Gleaner*. It was a very large paper compared with the wartime papers of the UK, and with each copy, you got a comic which was several pages thick, full of cartoon strips, etc. The local brew was a beer called Red Stripe. I found it drinkable when served ice cold but most vile when not. There were many varieties of rum, all very cheap. The favourite was one called Sugar Loaf, which was 4 shillings and 6 pence (old money) for the bottle (the Sugar Loaf Mountain being one of the highest peaks in the Blue Mountains).

Many of the stores made up food parcels of items that were impossible to get, or were in short supply, back home in the UK. From a price list you could choose the size of parcel you wished to send, give the shop-keeper the recipient's address, and money for the parcel and, before you knew it, there would be a letter from home saying, "Thank you for the parcel! We are really enjoying it!" My father's favourite was the jars of rum-flavoured marmalade. There was often a request to please send another jar! Every conscript (National Service man, that is) was given a Demob Group Number. This number was to be used when the time came for demobilization. How that number was achieved, it never was really explained to us, but we believed the top number was 100. Each conscript was dealt with individually, one unit for each month's service, extra units for service outside the UK, extra points on top of this for each month in a battle zone. The units were then added together and subtracted from 100, giving the conscript his demob number. So, it was not always first in, first out. My demob number was 55.

When the time came for me to leave Jamaica, the conscripts in Group 62 were already being demobbed back home in the UK. The reason for the delay in getting us demobbed was that the army was dependent on booking any spare berths on the one or two banana boats that carried a few paying passengers sailing for a port in the UK. Then, it would only be two or three spare berths so, getting anyone due for demob back to the UK, took time.

One day, my name, with three others, came up on battalion orders saying that in a few days we would be returning to the UK. It gave a list of equipment we were to return to the stores, and a list of what we would take with us. The next few days my heart was full of joy and, for the first time in my life, and probably the last time, I was really looking forward to seeing some winter weather. We were to sail for the port of Avonmouth on board the banana boat 'M. U. Bayano'. As the time approached for me to leave Jamaica, the joy that I once experienced turned to a certain feeling of sadness. Here I was, leaving men whom I held in the highest esteem. Living together for over three years, the friendship runs so deep. From the beaches and battlefields of Normandy to the sunshine of the Caribbean, we all had been a happy family, helping and caring for one another, often in very difficult conditions. But, as Mr Partridge, the builder, once said on sacking a long-serving worker, "Even the best of friends must part, Fred."

So, it was with a certain amount of sadness that I was leaving the island that had been my home for so long but looking forward to being a civilian once again, and to some good home-cooking. I seem to remember that the voyage took about ten days. As we sailed up the Bristol Channel, we were followed by many porpoises; they looked as though they were playing leap-frog with one another, as they rose and fell back into the water. In the evening before the morning when we were to disembark, a crew member brought a stem of bananas to our cabin for us to share and to take with us. They were large and as green as grass and as hard as bullets. In the morning, we disembarked, said thank you to the crew, and said farewell. We were then put on a train for Aldershot where the demob centre was. Arriving there, we handed in the remainder of our army issue and picked up our civilian clothes: shoes, three-piece suit, hat or cap. So, in army slang, I was now "Bowler-Hatted!"

Gerald, 1945

Chapter 10

Home Again

It was really good to be home and at last to feel the invigorating air of an English winter. I was left very much on my own as my two mates, being a couple of years younger, were still away doing their National Service, Tony in the RAF and Herbie in the army. After a few weeks at home, meeting people and catching up on things, I began to feel it was time to get a job of work and, not really knowing what sort of job I would be interested in, I visited Cirencester Labour Exchange where they said that there was a labourer's job vacant at what is now called by the nickname of 'The Burnt House' at Sapperton. It was a large gentleman's residence and it had a thatched roof which caught fire one Sunday morning while the tenants were at church and so the whole house had to be rebuilt, the roof this time being replaced with stone tiles. Orchard and Peer of Stroud were the builders and the foreman in charge of the work was my future father-in-law, though I had no idea at that time. His name was Cyril Truman.

Pay day in those days was on a Friday. One Friday, when Mr Orchard paid me, he asked me to go on the following Monday to King's Farm at Tunley for a few days to help

Stan Harrison, the carpenter, who was to hang and fix new
doors and posts to the stone barn, my job being to dig the
post holes and help lift the doors up and down. It was here
that I first met Gladys, my future wife, who was working on
the farm for Harry Finch. We straight away started a friendship. There was very little time off for either of us in those
days, but what time we did have together we spent walking
in the woods or along the path beside the disused canal,
having a drink at the Nelson Inn at Far Oakridge with the
friendly landlord, Irishman Larry Connors and his wife.

By the middle of 1948, the job at The Burnt House was
getting up together so Mr Orchard offered me a job in
Stroud which I considered far too far to travel on my bicycle
from Duntisbourne. So, I gave in my notice, leaving on the
Friday. The following Monday, I started work for Cazer
Securities, a firm from Birmingham who had the contract to
lay water mains from the reservoir at Birdlip to the villages
of Brimpsfield, Elkstone, Syde and Winstone. I am afraid
that there was not much security in this firm as, after
working for them for a few weeks, they went bankrupt,
meaning that I lost a week's pay, plus holiday pay. (I still
have the letter from the Official Receiver saying that I
would be paid as soon as there were funds available, but it
seems that there never were any funds.) We had just got to
the Syde turning on the A417, when all work had to stop;
so there is a length of water mains there that owes me a
week's wages.

So it was then back to the Labour Exchange, where I was
offered a job with a firm called Ankerdine, a firm doing
public works, new roads, sewers and water mains, most of
the work being in north Wiltshire, down as far as Devizes.
The work was hard and the hours were long. This, plus the
fact that I had to cycle to and from Cirencester, night and

morning from Duntisbourne. Long hours and so much trav-
elling meant that Gladys and I were seeing less and less of
each other. Being young, and in no hurry to settle down, we
parted the best of friends.

Chapter 11

Catching up on my Youth

(and a Broken Engagement)

It was then that I tried to catch up on my youth that the army had robbed me of. The Duntisbourne branch of the British Legion had thrown out a challenge to the North Cerney branch to a game of cricket on Duntisbourne cricket ground at the Five Mile House. The game was to be played one evening, though being a member I was unable to play, as working late the game would have been half over before I could get there. The evening of the cricket match, having finished my meal, I rode on my cycle up to the cricket ground to add my support to the many supporters. "Who was this young lady who was stood way out on her own, looking lonely?" I thought as I walked over to make conversation. She told me that her name was Nell Goode, that she lived with her parents at Warren's Gorse and that she was here to watch her brother, Richard, who was playing for North Cerney. The game over, most of the players and spectators retired to the Five Mile House for some liquid refreshment, but Nell said that she would be going straight

Gerald, 1946

home so, with nothing to do, I said, "I will see you home, if that is all right?"

This was to be a long and happy friendship. As the weeks and months passed, we saw more and more of each other; our interests were very much the same. We both loved cycling, walking, and the occasional visit to the cinema. As the months turned into years, we grew very fond of each other, and talked about spending our life together. She said that she was looking forward to the day when she could get married and was hoping to have four children which, she declared, was the ideal family. Having come from a large family, I could not go along with this, especially as things were at present, with the ever-increasing cost of living, which seemed, then, to have no end. So it was with the blessing of Nell's family, but much against my mother's wishes, that Nell and I got engaged.

It was after a few months that everything seemed to go

wrong. Nell seemed to change. She wanted to dominate my life, and became very demanding as to the who's and what for. Little arguments became much bigger, followed by a jolly good row. After giving our relationship a thorough good think-over, I decided it was better to part now, on friendly terms, than to part during married life. So, one night I explained to Nell how I saw the situation at present and, in the future, if ever we got married. Of course, it was very upsetting for Nell, as it was for myself, as I did think a lot of her but my inner self told me that I was doing the right thing, upsetting as it was. As a token of our friendship, and to prove that we were parting as friends, I told Nell to keep the engagement ring. It was hers to do whatever she wished to do with it. As expected, her family were very upset at our parting, but from my mother, there was no comment.

Chapter 12

My Working Life as a Roof Tiler

Having had several jobs on leaving the army, it was in 1953 that I decided it was time for me to learn a trade. As a schoolboy I had always been interested and fascinated by the stone tilers and plasterers working on the buildings in my home village. Then, the two trades were the job of one man. The trade was known as a Slatter and Plasterer. This is the trade I decided I would like to take up. So I went to Birdlip to have a chat with Martin Partridge, the founder of the building firm of M. J. Partridge Ltd., explaining to him as to what I wanted to do and agreeing terms. He said, "Start as soon as you like."

At the time, the firm was completely reroofing Woodfield House in Caudle Green, so this is where I was sent. The tiler in charge was Fred Waine, who had been with the firm from its very early days. Fred was a small man, but a real master at any form of plastering and any type of roofing. I was to spend the next seven years working under Fred's guidance. Suffering from severe bouts of arthritis and painful hip joints, he was forced into retirement in 1960, plunging me into the deep end, so to speak.

In those days, there was a lot more skill in dressing tiles. Tiles were cut and shaped with a dressing hammer, and holes were made in the tiles with a tile pick. These tile picks were made by a blacksmith out of large worn-out flat files or rasps, bent into the shape of a boomerang and drawn out to a sharp point at either end. These were then slotted into a purpose-made wooden handle. When one end of the tile pick was worn blunt, it was easy to knock it out and slot the other one in. When both ends of the pick were worn blunt, they would be taken to the blacksmith who again would draw them out to a sharp point. Making a tile pick was an art in itself. The point had to be soft, so as not to bend, but not too hard that they would snap off. There were very few blacksmiths who could get these tile picks just right, the main fault being that they would get them too hard, making them very brittle so that at the first tap, the point would break off.

Ray Barrett of Winstone was a real master in the art of tool-dressing. Tradesmen from a wide area would bring cold chisels, tile picks and dressing hammers to his forge to be dressed, such was his reputation. Today, if a tile needs to be dressed or shaped, it is done with an electric stone saw and the hole made by an electric drill and mason master, taking away, to my mind, much of the character of a stone tile roof.

Being a Cotswold stone tiler for many years, I would like to mention some of the buildings that I have worked on and some of the characters I have met along the way.

We reroofed much of Miserden Park and many of the estate cottages, as well as St Andrew's Church. We also did the church of the Holy Trinity in Watermoor, Cirencester, and Saul Church, down by the Severn. Here, elevations that could be seen from the road were retiled in stone tiles, the remainder of the elevations being done in Bridgewater handmade Roman clay tiles. They said at the time that these were the last of the handmade tiles to be produced before switching to machine-made tiles. These needed to be handled with great care as they were easily chipped.

Life in the villages down by the Severn seemed different to life on the hills. A local would often call in during our lunch break for a chat. I remember him telling us that he did not have a fridge and that they would put the meat and dairy produce in a container and lower it down the well which was by the back door and that, even on the hottest of summer days, they would keep as fresh, if not fresher, than they would in a fridge.

Next, we go to Bishop's Cleeve church, where it was a major roofing job, all in stone tiles. The problem with a job like this is that the church, being in a very heavy populated area, there are many funerals, during which all work would have to stop; so, when estimating for the contract, it would also mean estimating how many funerals there would be during the period of work.

There is a little story here: one morning, a man in working clothes, and looking very much like a builder, came to me and explained that the gutter in his cottage was blocked and that his ladder was not long enough to reach where it was blocked, and could he borrow one of our ladders for five minutes, his cottage being just round the corner. Pointing to a 27-rung ladder, he said, "That ladder would be ideal." I said, "If it's only for 5 minutes, take it." Picking the ladder up, he thanked me saying, "I will be back in 5 minutes," but as soon as he had gone through the churchyard gate I knew that I had been conned. The next worry was what sort of mood would Mr Partridge be in when I got back to the office to explain. Entering his office, he said, "Yes, Gerald, what is it?" I then went on to explain about the ladder and to my great relief he said, "Don't worry. The man may return it by morning. There are good people, as well as bad." But it was never returned.

I also had the job of retiling Witcombe church. The church tower was also tiled in stone tiles, though hidden behind parapet walls. The caretaker here was an elderly gentleman called Harry Hayward, a farmer who lived opposite the church. Telling mother where I was working, and about Harry, she said that as a young schoolgirl she had been sweet on Harry!

We also had the job of reroofing the sanctuary of Painswick parish church, where there was no access into the roof space from inside the church, the only way being through the roof from the outside. Someone decided that it would be a good idea to put a time capsule in the roof space before the last of the tiles was nailed into place, so that one day someone would find out what life was like in the last quarter of the 20th century.

We retiled much of Ewen Manor for Colonel Gibbs who told us that we were "*Very* expensive guests!"

A roof that I retiled on my own with the help of Albert, my labourer, was Butler's Farm House, at Colesborne, the home of the well-known Communist, Wogan Philipps who, on the death of his father, became Lord Milford. A couple of days after we had started the job, Wogan came to me complaining about the dust we were making, saying, "You wouldn't make that dust if you were working in London." My reply was, "I'm not working in London", whereby he said, "It's a good job you're not!" I then went on to explain to him that it was almost impossible to take an old roof off without making some dust and if he wanted the work done he would have to put up with it for a while and that we would make no more dust than we could help. Wogan accepted my explanation and all the time we were there he was most amicable, telling us to use the farm-workers' rest room at break times. The rest room was a small room in one of the farm buildings, with several chairs, and a table on which there was always a copy of *The Daily Worker*.

Wogan would also make us tea at break times, when he would stand outside the kitchen door and shout, in a loud voice, "Tea is ready!" Some days, he would spend time in his studio, painting in oils. Most Fridays, he would disappear, the farm foreman telling us that he was gone to Birmingham to the Longbridge motor works to speak to the workers and to hand out leaflets. Some weeks after we had finished the job at Butler's Farm, I got back to the yard at Birdlip and Mr Partridge said, "I had a gentleman in here this morning singing your praises!" It was Mr Philipps. He had gone to Birdlip to settle his account and to tell Mr Partridge how pleased he was with all the work we did.

Some months later, I was working in Rendcomb village when Wogan drove by in his car. He spotted me, stopped his car, got out and walked across the road, asking how things were and how was I. Years later, Mrs Jackson would tell me little things about Wogan, giving me a newspaper cutting of a report on his death and funeral.

We also did a lot of roofing at Stowell Park for Lord Vestey, including the large barn opposite Yanworth church which, I understand, they now use for various functions.

Reroofing a converted farm building which had been made into living accommodation in the village centre of Upper Slaughter was real interesting. It was the height of the summer holiday season while we were there and we were quite an attraction for many of the visitors. You could always pick out the Americans and Japanese from the rest of the tourists as they were the ones with the most cameras hanging round their necks, the Japanese trying to outdo the Americans on this score. When we were nailing the tiles to the batten, one American, not seeing there was already a hole in each tile, and watching me nailing tiles to the battens, shouted up to me, "That sure must be some nail to be able to drive it through a piece of stone as easy as that!" Another American lady asked if she could come into the yard where the tiles were stacked as she would like to touch and feel them! The only time that I worked with newly-quarried tiles was on a new roof at Througham Manor in 1954, customers much preferring the second-hand tiles which were already tried and tested and which, in my early days, became very valuable. Today they are like gold dust! The firm of M. J. Partridge employed several tilers, but we worked mostly in pairs, plus labourers. On the smaller jobs, it would be one tiler and one labourer. Roofing was an outdoor life, one in which you could be baked in some summers and frozen to death in some winters but, for all this, I enjoyed the life, never once regretting the day I decided to become a Cotswold Stone Tiler.

Chapter 13

My Parents

I feel that I must write about my parents to let my grand-children, Stephen and Emily, know a little about their great-grandparents. As I have already written, my father was born in Forfar, County Angus, on the 17th of July 1881. It was while working on the railway in Stirling that my father got dismissed for playing cards during works time. And it was then that he must have decided to enlist in the regular army, joining up in the R.H.A. (Royal Horse Artillery). A mention at this point: his siblings had already emigrated to Canada, which seemed to be quite a regular thing among families in the early part of the 20th century.

It was while he was billeted in Edinburgh Castle that he had an operation to remove his appendix, which was not a common or easy operation then, as it is today. He would often tell us children that after King Edward VII, he was the second person in the country to have such an operation! Right or wrong? Or just leg pull? But I do know that he had the most unsightly scar across his stomach. In comparison, I had my appendix removed in the 1970's, and the scar is almost invisible.

My mother was born on the 7th December 1894, in the

Father in uniform, *c.* 1914

parish of Cowley. At the age of 13, she was sent away to work in domestic service, as it was called in those days. It was while working in Fleet in Hampshire that she met my father; I do not know in what year. They were married at St Michael's Church, Brimpsfield on the 8th April, 1916, when my father was home on leave from France where he served for most of the war. I remember mother telling us that two days after their wedding, my father had to return to France; they walked from Birdlip to the tram terminus at Hucclecote to catch a tram into Gloucester. They were walking through slushy snow on the roads and pavements. My father's first job on leaving the army was working on horse-drawn timber carriages for a firm called Packers of Cheltenham. There are family photos of him hauling timber off the Duke of Marlborough's estate at Blenheim. So Stephen and Emily, that is just a short history of your great-grandparents.

Mother, *c.* 1916

Chapter 14

My Grandparents

My grandfather, William Coles, died at the age of 79 years on the 1st March 1948; my grandmother died three years later, on the 14th May, 1951, at the age of 83 years. Both were buried in the family plot in the churchyard of St Peter's, Duntisbourne Abbots. The death of my grandparents was a sad and upsetting time for me as I thought so much of them both. Life was not going to be quite the same without them. I was so fortunate to have such wonderful, loving grandparents. The love and affection that they gave to all their grandchildren is something I will never forget, something that will live in my memory forever. And, though times were hard, and they had but very little, Gran (as my grandmother liked to be called), would always find something tasty to give us whenever we called on her, be it a sweet or a slice of her homemade cake.

My grandparents had lived in a cottage at Duntisbourne Abbots with their daughter, Bertha, who had bought the cottage so that she could look after them in their final years. When my aunt Bertha died, in 1981 at the age of 81, having never married, my grandparents' home was split up and the cottage was sold. My grandfather, at the time of his

My grandparents

marriage, was working as under-keeper to his father, who was the head-keeper on the Eyford estate, near Stow-on-the-Wold. My grandfather had a pet canary whose name was Tweet. When my grandparents set up home together, my grandfather took Tweet with him. When, eventually, Tweet died, my grandmother took him to a taxidermist, had him preserved and mounted in a glass dome, looking very life-like. Imagine my delight when I was given Tweet! Today, Tweet has pride of place on the top of the chest on the landing, a reminder of all the happy times I spent with my wonderful grandparents.

Though my aunt's name is inscribed on the family head-stone in St. Peter's churchyard, she was cremated at Gloucester Crematorium, and her ashes were scattered there, in the Garden of Remembrance.

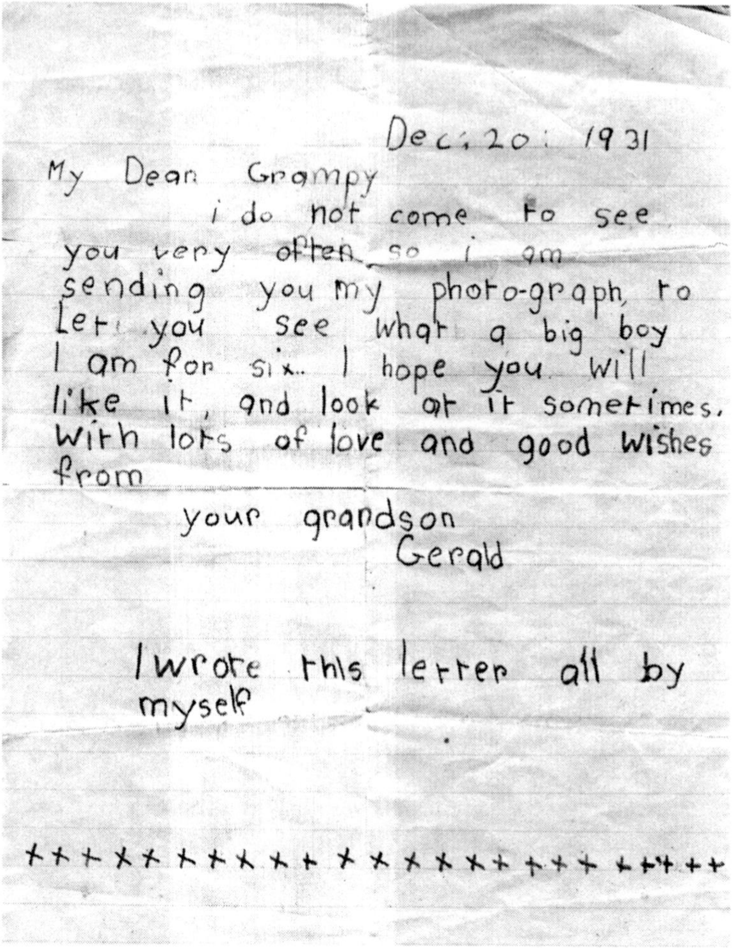

Dec. 20. 1931

My Dear Grampy

i do not come to see you very often so i am sending you my photo-graph to let you see what a big boy I am for six. I hope you will like it, and look at it sometimes. With lots of love and good wishes from

your grandson

Gerald

I wrote this letter all by myself

xxxxxxxxxxxxxxxxxxxxxxxxx

Letter to grandparents from grandson Gerald, 1931

Chapter 15

An old Friendship Rekindled

("And the rest," as they say, "is history.")

Having parted from Nell, I now found myself very much on my own, as my two school mates were away doing their National Service, Herbie in the army, Tony in the RAF. Cycling to work in Cirencester, six miles to and from, six days a week, in all winds and weather, I decided it was time to update my means of transport. So, one Saturday afternoon, I went to Gloucester in search of a motorcycle that would suit my needs, calling at Mead and Tomkinson, motor-cycle dealers. I found just the right one and, most important of all, one at the right price, as money was still in short supply. The motorcycle was a 197cc Ambassador; the price was £85. This was going to be the start of a love affair with motorcycles. Any spare time that I had at weekends was spent attending motor cycle trials at scrambles, at various venues in the county, and beyond.

It was coming back from one such trip one Sunday evening that I caught up with Gladys's parents who were

out on their Sunday evening walk. Stopping to have a word
with them, they invited me back to their cottage for supper.

During supper, I was talking over past times with Gladys's
Mum and Dad when the door opened and in walked
Gladys, arriving home after her night out. It was the first
time that I had seen her for several years and I at once made
up my mind that she was the woman who I would love to
share the rest of my life with. The question was: did she feel
the same about me?

When it came time for me to leave, Gladys said that she
would hold the gate open for me while I got my motorcycle
out onto the road. It was while she was holding the gate
open that I plucked up courage to ask her for a date for the
following weekend. To this she replied, "Yes." So, we
arranged to meet up after work the following Saturday.

This was to be the start of our renewed friendship, one
which would end in marriage the following year. It was
early summer. Gladys's time off was very restricted as her
job meant that she had to help with the haymaking and
harvest. I was also working long hours in my job but, what
time we did have together, we spent walking in the beautiful countryside around Tunley. Along the disused canal
towpath was one of our favourite walks, and also, through
Siccaridge, where the Lily-of-the-Valley grew and where we
could see the nests built of twigs by the wood ants. On our
way back, we would often call in at The Nelson Inn at Far
Oakridge for a glass of beer and a chat with the friendly
landlord, Irishman Larry Connors.

So, summer turned to autumn, and autumn to winter;
then came the New Year. It was then that we decided to get
married in the November. There was no proposal or engagement, just a decision to get married. I do not remember the
actual moment but, as the saying goes, "the rest is history."

In March, 1953, I left the firm of Ankerdine, getting a job at M. J. Partridge, builders, of Birdlip, where I was to work until I retired in 2000.

As Gladys and I had decided that we would get married, where would we find somewhere to live? Knowing that Mr Partridge had two empty cottages, I asked him if I could rent one of them. He offered me the one called The Cottage on the Ridge: rather a romantic name for a small cottage with two up and one down, and no bathroom, that needed a bit of work doing to it. So, all the spare time that I had before our wedding day was spent working on the cottage. I well remember how awful the weather was: it seemed to do nothing but rain, day after day.

When it came to the question of the rent I was to pay, Mr Partridge said that it would be £50 a year. (£4 a month, paid monthly to his rent collector, who was his daughter, Joan, and with £6 payable on the last month of the year.) He then had the cheek to say, "I won't charge you any rent for the weeks that you have been working on the cottage." I should have replied, "No, but I was going to charge *you* for my labours."

Chapter 16

Our Wedding

Having found somewhere to live, it was now time to start making wedding arrangements. The wedding day was to be the 27th November, 1954, at St Mary's, Edgeworth. The Reverend Anthony Thorpe, Vicar of Miserden with Edgeworth, would officiate. Gladys would be given away by her father; her three sisters would be bridesmaids, my brother Philip would be my best man, and the reception would be held in the Village Reading Room. Larry Connors from the Nelson Inn at Far Oakridge would provide the liquid refreshment.

The big day arrived. The weather no different from what it had been for the past few weeks: a dull, misty, cold November day but, at least it was not raining. We had hired a coach from Alex Cars of Baunton to bring relatives and friends from across the valley at Duntisbourne to the church.

The reception over, we were taken by taxi to our first home, having decided to honeymoon in Devon the next summer when, hopefully, the weather would be fine and warm.

Our wedding, 1954

Our Golden Wedding, 2004

Chapter 17

Move to Caudle Green

So, after a week off, it was back to work. The following year, Mr Partridge sent me to work at Woodfield House, Caudle Green, where they were re-roofing the whole house. Mrs Benson, and her two unmarried daughters, were living in the house at the time: Miss Mary and Miss Madge, as they always liked to be called.

One day, Miss Mary, the one that always seemed to be in charge, came to me and said that one of their cottages was becoming vacant and would I like to rent it? The cottage was the one in which we are still living and which, at that time, for whatever reason, was called Bird's Eye Cottage.

Miss Mary thought that this name was not appropriate to the cottage and renamed it Cow Dell Cottage, from where she said Caudle Green got its name.

So it was that we moved into our present cottage on the 8th October, 1955. The cottage then had a sitting-room, kitchen and bathroom downstairs, and two bedrooms. It had the quaintest staircase: the first two treads were out into the sitting-room, in front of the stairs door. The rest of the stairs were built in a circular fashion, anti-clockwise, each tread being triangular in shape, and each big enough to put two feet on at once. The whole of the staircase was made of polished elm wood.

This was a real palace to what we had at Birdlip, grateful as we were to Mr Partridge for starting us up in our first home. But no way could we turn down an offer as good as this. I agreed with Miss Mary to take the cottage. She fixed the rent at 12 shillings a week, paid monthly.

It was in 1958 that Mrs Benson died and that the Woodfield estate was sold, each tenant being given the chance to buy the cottage they were renting, except for Bird's Cottage, into which Miss Mary moved while having her house built in her paddock. She called the house Calley Close. (Miss Madge had already bought a house in Henley-on-Thames and had moved away).

The offer to buy our cottage was too good an offer to miss. With funds being low, it was a great worry but, with encouragement and help from mother and her great friend, George Newsham, chairman of the Holloway Friendly Society, we were able to take up a mortgage on our cottage. Looking back on those early years, the money concerned then would be pocket-money today, but to buy the cottage today, you would probably be talking 'telephone numbers', as the saying goes.

Cow Dell Cottage, Caudle Green [Photo: *Richard Beal*]

Chapter 18

Births of David and Richard (and Motorcycles)

Having had my first motorcycle for some time, and having passed my test for it, it was then that I decided that I would like something bigger and more powerful. So, one Saturday afternoon, I drove to Oxford to a motorcycle dealer by the name of Leytons. There, I spotted just the motorcycle that would suit my needs: it was an A.J.S. 350cc. A deal made, I drove it home. I well remember the worry that it gave my father to see a big and more powerful motorcycle. I could understand his concern and his worry about me as, at that time, motorcycle accidents were quite common, many with a fatal consequence. Our next motorcycle was a BSA C11G. This was a less powerful bike but a much newer and more up-to-date model. It was this motorcycle that would take Gladys and me on our honeymoon to Paignton the following August. I well remember how well it behaved, getting us there and back with no trouble.

It was in 1956 that Gladys became pregnant and on the

29th January 1957, David was born in the Quern's Maternity Hospital, Cirencester. Like everyone else, Mrs Benson, who lived at Woodfield, wanted to see our new-born son but, being confined to a wheel-chair, there was no way that she could come to our cottage, so we took David round to see her. On leaving, she gave David an egg and sixpence and some salt. As she was from Devon, we took this as being an old Devonshire custom. We translated it to mean the egg for fertility, sixpence for wealth, and salt for long life. We have never really known the answer.

Now we had David, the motorcycle was not much use to a family of three. Having no licence to drive a car, I was on the lookout for a (combination) motorcycle and side-car. In my summer holidays, I visited H and L, the motorcycle dealers of Stroud, where I spotted the very thing that I was looking for: a BSA M21, with a side-car. The side-car was a single-seater adult, so Gladys would have David on her lap.

The time was that David was getting bigger and Gladys was now expecting Richard. It was time to upgrade the side-car. So, we bought a new Watsonian child-adult side-car from Williams, the motorcycle dealers of Cheltenham. The accommodation in this side-car was Gladys in front, with David in his own little seat behind her. At first, David was very nervous on coming to a steep hill: he would completely disappear behind his mother's seat, appearing once again when we were on the level. Having driven a motorcycle for so long, to drive a motorcycle combination was quite a different cup of tea, always having to remember to accelerate when turning left, and to ease off the power when turning right.

What pleasure this motorcycle combination was to give us as a family! When I look back over our motorcycling days, I remember all those happy times: the places we visited, the many miles we travelled, not always without incident, I might add. I remember one time when, coming back from Cheltenham, on reaching the Green, I went up the bank, giving us all a scare. But, the most laughable incident now, but not then, was the afternoon that I tipped my sister-in-law, Joan, and her daughter, out of the side-car. Joan lived at Eastcombe, and to visit her mother, she would take the bus to Oakridge and walk the remainder of the journey to Tunley. This particular day, we were visiting my in-laws. When it came time for Joan to leave for home, I offered to take her all the way. Joan accepted the offer and everything went well until we got to Frith Hill. On negotiating the steepest part, I missed my gear and, before I could take evasive action, the combination ran back, mounting the steep bank and tipping Joan and her daughter out of the side-car. After getting the combination back on the road, and loading my passengers, we were once again mobile, a little shaken but none the worse. I never remember Joan riding in the side-car ever again after that episode.

The boys growing up, it was now time to upgrade our means of transport from three to four wheels, but first I must get a licence to drive a car, so I booked-in for lessons at the BSM in Cheltenham. My instructor was a very patient man by the name of David Turner. I remember the lessons were 12 shilling an hour, 60p in today's money. It was now a case of looking for a vehicle that we could afford. Cars were very expensive, even the older ones, and money was short. Eventually, I found a Thames Ford van at the right price. It had two seats in the front, David and Richard sitting on cushions in the back. We were now a complete family as we had room to take Sally, our Welsh collie, with us, too.

The boys growing bigger, it was then time to get a car

which would give them more comfort. So, our first motor-
car was a Morris Minor. What pleasure and trouble-free
motoring this little car gave us! We bought our first Volkswagen in the early 1970's. Having fallen in love with
Volkswagen, we have owned one ever since. Driving cars
has never given me the pleasure that I got from my motorcycling days; there was always so much comradeship among
the motorcycling fraternity.

Chapter 19

Life at Caudle Green

So, now is the time to write a little about my life in Caudle Green.

The whole of the field behind Caudle Farm had always been the allotments for the villagers of Syde and Caudle Green; but, by the time I came to the village, there were only five being worked. Mr Cox, our next door neighbour, had his allotment where the bungalow is now, the other four being over the wall by the bus-stop. The top right-hand one was worked by Bertie Locke, the bottom right by his father, Horace, the top left by Miss Benson, the bottom left being vacant. Miss Benson offered me the one that was vacant, the rent being 10 shillings a year (50p in today's money). Eventually, Miss Benson had her new house built (Calley Close), complete with kitchen garden. No longer needing the allotment, she told me to take it over, which I did. This, then, enabled me to keep a few hens to supply us with fresh eggs.

When Caudle Farm was sold to Mr Mills, Bertie and Horace Locke gave up their allotments, so the fence was moved up, me taking over the top two allotments. There, I cultivated until the year 2005, when I took up the fence to return the allotments back into the field.

Over the years, the allotment had given me much pleasure and an abundance of flowers and vegetables which I do miss. The allotment was always a place I could relax in, but I feel that I did the right thing, as I am not getting any younger.

It was in the summer of 1957, when Mr Evans of Caudle Green Farm now Caudle Green House, came along and asked me if I would give him a hand haymaking, nights and Saturdays. This I did, as extra cash was always helpful. Haymaking finished, he needed a hand with the harvest, so I gave a hand. This I continued to do until Mr Evans retired from farming. The haymaking and harvesting equipment in those days was a lot smaller and slower than those of the present day. Some years, the weather being bad, haymaking would run into harvest. Mr Evans always had the best equipment; he would say, "You can't afford to have machinery breakdowns when employing casual labour." Mr Evans was an expert at forecasting the weather, even several weeks ahead, having many sayings about it on which he based his forecast, and which I regret I never recorded.

I well remember one evening we were picking up bales in Penn Piece; it was quite late; the full moon was up; it was a lovely late Autumn evening. Mr Evans said that we were in for a dry spell of weather, "Look at the man in the moon. He is all smiles and he has got his mug of beer in his hand." And there, looking at the moon, we could see a large face with a large smile and beer froth running down the side of the mug. A sight like this has to be seen to be believed. Never have I seen anything like it since.

Mr Mills farmed Caudle Farm on which he kept a small herd of dairy cows, the milk from which he supplied the residents of the Green, the surplus being sent to Gloucester. Each customer put their jug or can on the dairy table. Mr

Mills would fill the can or jug with the required amount from the afternoon milking. This practice carried on for many years until such times as the Ministry of Food and Fisheries brought in the rule that all milk was to be sold in bottles which must carry the name of the producer and the name of the farm on which it was produced. Most of us got our milk from Mr Mills until he retired, eventually moving to a bungalow in South Cerney. Since then, various dairies have delivered milk to the Green, the one at the time of writing being Express Dairies from Gloucester.

Though Mr and Mrs Mills had no family, they were great with children. David and Richard spent a lot of time with Mr Mills, learning a lot from him as he was a wise man, a great countryman, never in a hurry, never in a bad mood. In today's terms, he would be described as very laid back. Mr Evans or Mr Hannis would cut his grass and make the hay, but he depended on after-tea labour to pick up his bales. Whether it was a good or bad hay-making season, Mr Mills

David and Richard tending Mrs Jackson's cattle with
Mr Mills, *c.* 1972

would just not come out to bale cart, even with rain threat-
ening, until he had listened to the Archers. But looking back
over the years, he got by as well as anyone else.

Mr Mills had many favourite sayings. Two of his
favourites were, "We all know what we want, but it is better
to make a study of what we can do without," and "Believe
nothing you hear and only half of what you see."

Chapter 20

Woodfield House, Caudle Green

It was in 1959 that the Hon. Pamela Jackson bought Woodfield House, Mrs Benson, the previous owner, having died there in 1958.

Mrs Jackson was one of the famous Mitford sisters. John Betjeman, who had wanted to marry her, wrote, "Pamela, the most rural of them all."

Before the actual move, some afternoons, Mrs Jackson would come and spend time in the garden. It was on one such afternoon that Mrs Jackson knocked on our cottage door, asking Gladys if she could come in and wash her hands. It was whilst washing her hands that she asked Gladys if she knew anyone who would help her [Mrs Jackson] in the garden at Woodfield. Gladys said that she would ask me and so, one evening, I met Mrs Jackson.

I knew at once on meeting her that she was a person whom I could get on with. Telling me what the job was and agreeing terms, I started looking after the gardens at Woodfield, never ever then thinking that fifty years later I would still be tending those same gardens!

Woodfield House, Caudle Green [Photo: *Frederica Freer*]

I found Mrs Jackson a very interesting person, her great love being her kitchen garden which she always enjoyed showing to her visitors. But sadly, in 1994, on a visit to London, she had a fall which brought about her death. She left Woodfield House to her niece, Lady Emma Tennant, the daughter of Deborah, now the Dowager Duchess of Devonshire.

On meeting Lady Emma, she asked me if I would be willing to continue looking after the gardens at Woodfield as I had done for Mrs Jackson but explaining that Woodfield would be let to a tenant. Having a great love of Woodfield, I was so pleased to be asked to carry on working there.

So ... here I am today, fifty years after first starting at Woodfield, still tending the gardens, perhaps a little slower but with just as much love and enthusiasm.

Chapter 21

Grandchildren

So it was that on 4th February 2002, that our first grandchild was born: a grandson, Stephen Richard. Then, on the 27th February, 2006, our granddaughter, Emily Jessica, was born.

It was some time after the birth of Emily that Mrs Freer, now the tenant of Woodfield, arrived at our cottage with a pen and writing pad and with the suggestion that me, being

Gerald with his grandchildren, Stephen and Emily Stewart, 2008
[Photo: *Frederica Freer*]

an octogenarian, she thought it would be a good idea if I wrote a little about my life as in all probability my grandchildren would grow up not knowing much about their grandfather. Me, I thought that this was an excellent idea. It has given me great pleasure to write a little about my first 80 years. I hope that when Stephen and Emily are old enough to read and understand what I have written, they will get pleasure and gain some knowledge about their grandfather.

Myself, I have had a great life being married to my wife, Gladys, for fifty-four years. In that time, Gladys has been my rock, someone whom I can always depend on in time of need. She has given me two sons, David and Richard, for which I am thankful. As Mr Cove, a farmer from Winstone once told me, "You can never have another mother but you can always have another wife. But, if the one you have is a good one, then look after her." Taking Mr Cove's advice, I have done my best to look after Gladys.

Looking back over the last eighty or so years, I have had a good life, being brought up with my three brothers and three sisters in a house where discipline was paramount to my parents but love was there, too, in abundance. I also had grandparents, whom I simply adored. From my schoolboy days until the present time, I have made many friends from all walks of life but, alas, many are no longer here but, then ... that's life.

Lightning Source UK Ltd.
Milton Keynes UK
28 October 2009

145477UK00001B/7/P